Darwin

and the voyage of the Beagle

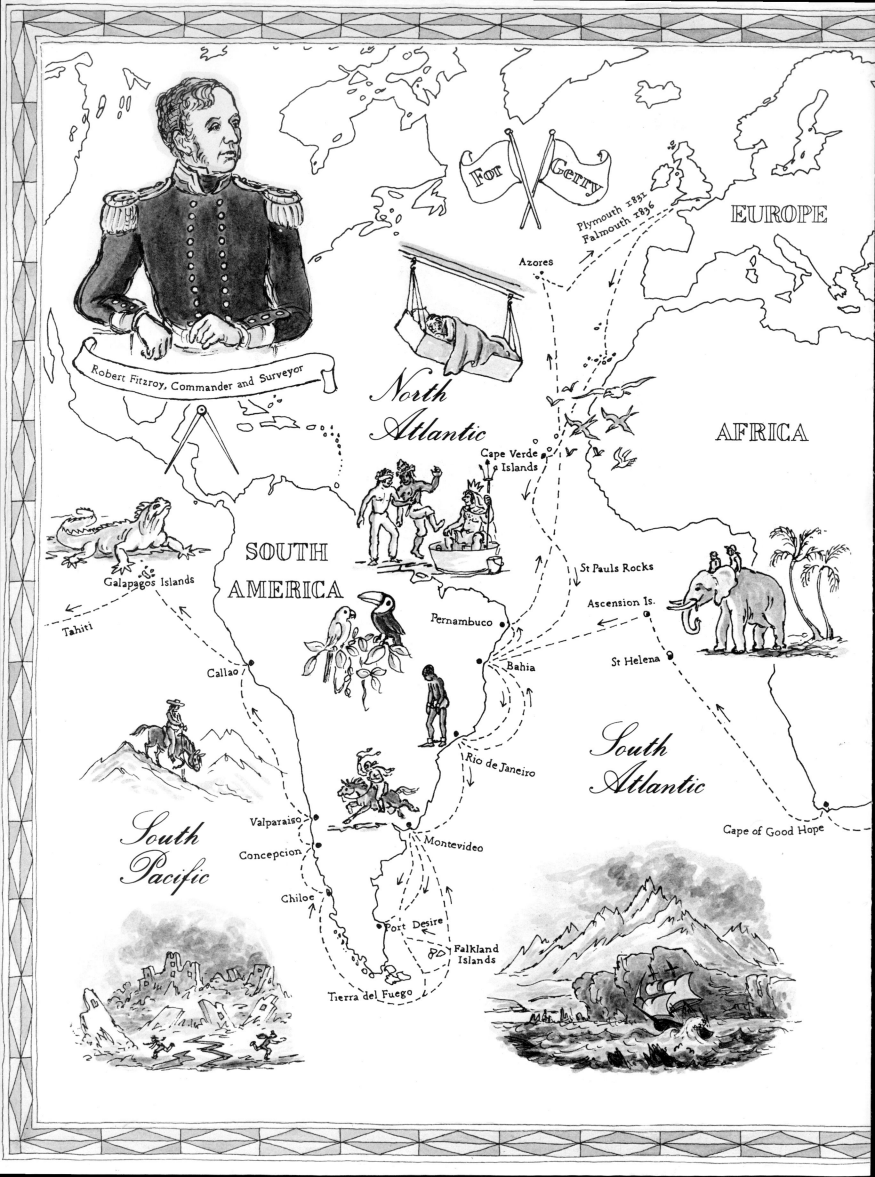

Robert Fitzroy, Commander and Surveyor

For Gerry

Plymouth 1831
Falmouth 1836

EUROPE

AFRICA

Azores

North
Atlantic

Cape Verde
Islands

St Pauls Rocks

Ascension Is.

St Helena

SOUTH
AMERICA

Galapagos Islands

Tahiti

Pernambuco

Bahia

South
Atlantic

Callao

Rio de Janeiro

South
Pacific

Valparaiso

Concepcion

Montevideo

Cape of Good Hope

Chiloe

Port Desire

Falkland
Islands

Tierra del Fuego

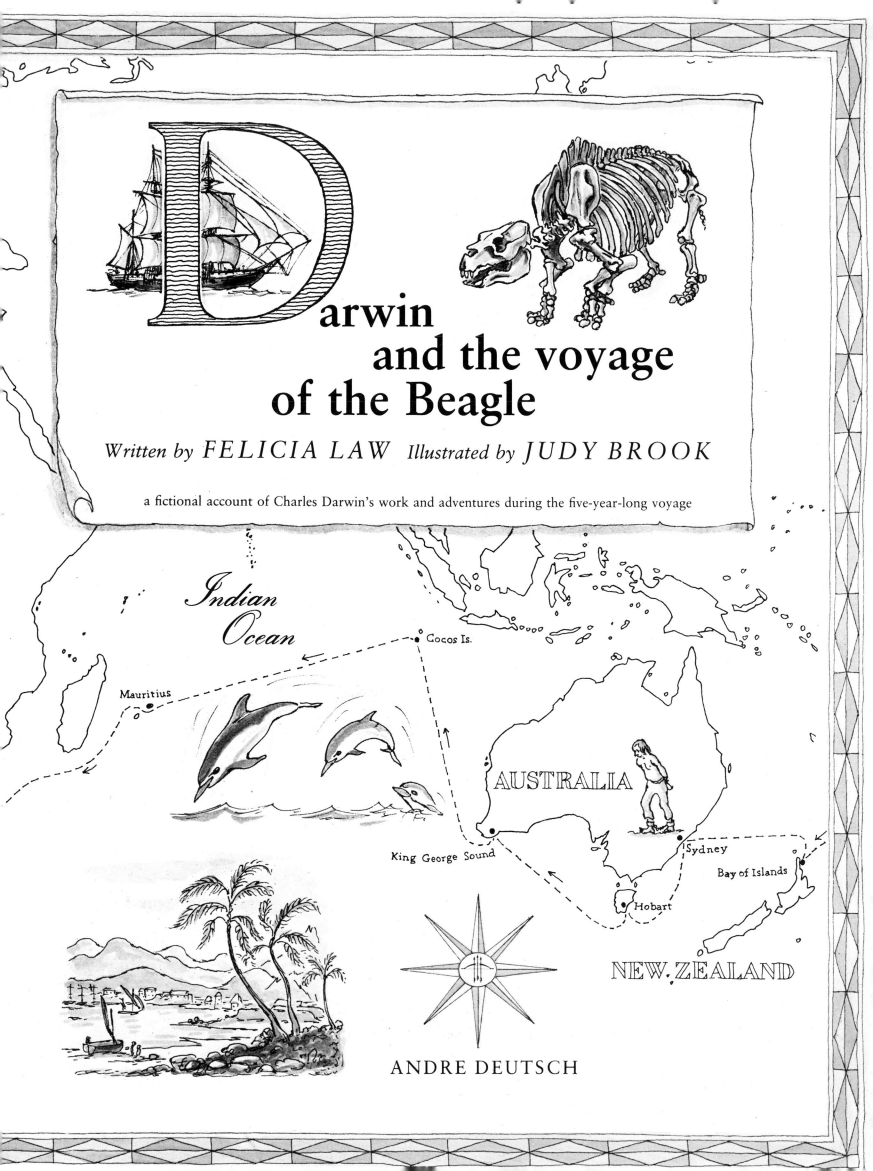

Darwin and the voyage of the Beagle

Written by *FELICIA LAW*   Illustrated by *JUDY BROOK*

a fictional account of Charles Darwin's work and adventures during the five-year-long voyage

Indian Ocean

Cocos Is.

Mauritius

AUSTRALIA

King George Sound

Sydney

Bay of Islands

Hobart

NEW ZEALAND

ANDRE DEUTSCH

First published in Great Britain 1985
André Deutsch Limited
105 Great Russell Street, London WC1

Text copyright © 1982 by Felicia Law
Illustrations copyright © 1982 Judy Brook
Illustrations in Ben's sketchbook copyright © 1982 Thomas Irvine
Book designed by Pat Schleger

Printed in Great Britain by McCorquodale (Scotland) Limited

British Library Cataloguing in Publication Data
Law, Felicia
   Darwin and the voyage of the Beagle.
   1. Beagle *(Ship)* — Juvenile literature
   2. Scientific expeditions — Juvenile
   literature
   I. Title
   508.3   QH11

   ISBN 0-233-97482-2

Library of Congress Number
84-071817

The following books have been invaluable:

The Beagle Record · *edited by R D Keynes · Cambridge University Press*
Darwin and the Beagle · *Alan Moorhead · Penguin Books*
The Origin of Species · *Charles Darwin · Everyman's University Library, J M Dent*
The Autobiography and Selected Letters of Charles Darwin · *Edited by F Darwin · Dover Publications*
Voyage of the Beagle · *Charles Darwin · Everyman's Library, J M Dent*

Acknowledgements

The chart on page 13 of the port and river of Santa Cruz was made by the officers of HMS Beagle for an atlas of 44 charts of the east and west coasts of South America, published circa 1845. By kind permission of the National Maritime Museum, London.

The engraving on pages 48/49 is taken from the 1889 Minerva edition of Charles Darwin's Journal.

The 1840 portrait of Charles Darwin on page 1 is by George Richmond. Reproduced by kind permission of George Darwin Esq, the Royal College of Surgeons and the curators of Down House, Kent.

In researching the illustrations for this book Judy Brook was given generous help by the following museums and some departments in particular:

British Museum (Natural History)

Paleontology

Entomology

Marine Biology

Crustacea

Mollusca

Natural History Museum, Tring

Geological Museum

National Maritime Museum, Greenwich

Judy Brook would also like to thank the Geographical Society, the British Museum library and Chiswick public library.

The author would like to acknowledge help from John Bartholomew of John Bartholomew and Son Ltd, Edinburgh

*On the 27th of December 1831, a small, three-masted brig set
sail from Plymouth on the first leg of its journey round the world.
The ship was bound for South America, the South Seas, Australia,
New Zealand and Mauritius; its mission – to chart the shoreline
and coastal waters of important landmarks en route.*

*On board were the captain and his crew, a motley assortment
of men, including a surgeon, an instrument maker, a missionary,
an artist, a naturalist and three natives from the Island of Tierra
del Fuego.*

*The ship was the Beagle and its captain, Robert Fitzroy. The
mission was no different from the navigational tasks carried out
by many ships at the time.*

*But almost as an afterthought, one more passenger was invited on
board. He was an easy-going, intelligent young man, not especially
learned or serious-minded, but a cheerful companion with whom
Captain Fitzroy hoped to while away the long months at sea.*

*But the young man contributed far more than that. His name was
Charles Darwin and his researches and studies led to a voyage of
fresh discovery not just about lands and peoples far away,
but about ourselves; our behaviour, our instincts, and our origins.*

*When Darwin published his ideas as to the way in which animals,
plants and insects had slowly developed and changed over the
millions of years of the world's geological formation, he shocked
many people who believed unfailingly in the Bible's teachings.
Since God had made all living things, they argued how could
Darwin substantiate his theory of gradual evolution?*

*It was not easy. It took years and years of acute observation,
experiment and trial and error to gather enough scientific
evidence, and on that day in December 1831, the work was only
just about to begin . . .*

In writing this account of Darwin's activities throughout the long
voyage of the Beagle, the author has drawn widely from the published
journals, diaries and letters of both Charles Darwin and
Captain Robert Fitzroy. The character of the cabin boy, Ben Sweet,
is invented, but it was not uncommon for boys of Ben's age to sail
in naval ships at this time; indeed, it is recorded that six boys
sailed with Captain Fitzroy on the Beagle's voyage round the world.
Morever, it is in keeping with all that we know of Darwin later,
as a fond and caring father, that he would befriend a child who was
unhappy and whose talents were being wasted.

"... forty-six, forty-seven, forty-eight."

Darwin's toe came to an abrupt halt against the solid planking of the fo'c'sle. This was it then! For the next two years, if not longer, his daily constitutional would be confined to forty-eight paces along the starboard deck and forty-eight paces back along the port. How would he cope, he wondered, being an active person who loved nothing better than to tramp the countryside on walking holidays, or roam acres of forest and moorland on a day's shooting excursion? Darwin's mind flashed to the cramped cabin below the coachhouse which he shared with Captain Fitzroy. Here, eight weeks previously, Fitzroy had delivered

his welcome, indicating the lockers and chests where Darwin might stow his belongings and advising him on the best way to string his hammock for comfort.

The thought of the glorious adventure ahead lifted Darwin's spirits. It was a truly unexpected opportunity that had come his way. If only they could get underway. For weeks now the Beagle had lain to in the shelter of Devonport harbour, delayed firstly as the carpenters and chandlers laboured unhurriedly on the necessary repairs and refurbishings, and now by violent December gales that had twice thwarted their efforts to set sail.

Darwin's eyes moved restlessly over the brig. From his vantage point on the fo'c'sle he could survey the activity on the deck below; several ratings greasing the hawser, the master's mate giving a final spit and polish to the wheel, the bosun checking the deck rigging, late deliveries of cargo disappearing down the hatches. Shielding his eyes against the biting winter wind, Darwin gazed upwards, seeking out the whistling seaman whose repetitive ditty rang down from the mizzen mast. Yes, there he was, a small figure on the far spar, struggling to lash down a loose sail flap against the teasing wind. Darwin watched for a while, his gaze wandering over the rippling swell of canvas sail, from the foremast sails high above the prow to the main mast amidships and the mizzen mast far astern.

Suddenly Darwin's upturned face caught the full force of a sharp object plummeting from above. He winced at the sharp pain, not understanding its cause; then, noticing a crayon lying nearby, looked up angrily to scold the careless offender.

A young lad was balanced astride the yard arm some ten metres from the deck. He must have been there, lodged silently above Darwin's head, for some time, for no rustle or movement had betrayed his presence.

"Hey!" called Darwin. "Down you come boy, and give an account of yourself."

Even from so great a distance, Darwin could sense the boy's sulky defiance, for he made no effort to hurry down, picking his footholds on the rigging with an almost lazy swagger. At last he stood on the deck of the fo'c'sle and Darwin saw that he was a lad of about twelve, probably a stores' boy by his dress — a well-kneed pair of duck trousers and a faded blue short jacket. Darwin challenged the surly youth.

"Well, you're a fine marksman but no great hero when it comes to apologising, I see. Why the deuce didn't you shout to warn me? I suppose I should be grateful it wasn't a mallet.

The boy mumbled something, but Darwin had to lean forward to catch the words. "What was that?"

"I wasn't s'posed to be up there, I couldn't warn you."

"Which means you were up to some mischief, eh?"

"I wasn't up to nothing." The boy glowered defiantly, his body hunched and tense.

But no violence came from this quarter. The threat came from elsewhere.

"What's this, Sweet, beggin' yer pardon, Mister Darwin, you been annoyin' this gen'leman?" A heavy hand descended on the boy's shoulders, pushing him violently to one side, then serving a whiplash across the cheek. "You be a varmint, Sweet, no doubt about it, an idle, whinin' varmint. You can scarper off 'n hide all you likes, but I'll bash you into shape this trip if it's the last thing I do! There's work awaitin' ye, me son, same as ye crawled off 'n left your mates to do; so now I'll see you work twice as 'ard. Understand?"

A threatening fist sent the boy grappling down the steps and scurrying for the open door of the deck house. The quartermaster turned apologetically to Darwin and addressed him as one reasonable man to another.

"Six lads I got this voyage, sir, and none bin to sea afore now. An' that Sweet, 'e be the worst o' the lot. 'E be sly and work shy, a right ruffian in the making. Now if you'll pardon me I'd best be after him case 'e skulks away again."

The quartermaster ran his hands down his calico apron as if to smooth them for the angry fray to come and shuffled off. Darwin watched him go thoughtfully, then stooped to retrieve the offending crayon. In bending, his eye caught a folded leaf of paper lodged against the uneven boards, a torn wrapper from a biscuit chest. Curious, he opened it out. The crayon and paper had clearly served the same master, for sketched in sharp relief was one of the most skilful and dramatic drawings Darwin had ever seen, a lifelike impression of the sailor on the main mast posed against an angry, billowing sky. The boy was clearly a talented ruffian, if ruffian he was, thought Darwin, and he determined to find out more about the lad.

9

27th December 1831

A few days later, on the twenty-seventh of December 1831, the Beagle set sail at last. As the ship was loosed from its moorings, the crew manning the yards and hawsers bent and hauled on the ropes to the rhythm of the fife. The breeze caught each sail as it unfurled and the ship slid evenly from the shelter of the cliffs into the rolling swell of the open sea. Darwin stood on the deck, excited by the sudden activity on board. It seemed to him that every member of the crew sensed the stirrings of a grand adventure and they worked with unusual vigour and discipline, obeying to a man the precise signals of the coxswain's pipe.

After the long months of waiting, Captain Fitzroy and his officers were in celebratory mood when they dined that evening round the table in the gun room. A busy morning spent re-arranging his stowed possessions more firmly and enjoying the fresh air on deck had given Darwin an excellent appetite. He ate heartily, enjoying this first jolly encounter with men he would undoubtedly grow to know very well during the long voyage.

He rolled into his hammock elated and happy, only to wake a few hours later feeling sick and giddy. Before long his stomach had emptied itself and he lay hot and exhausted throughout the night, watching the stars through the skylight as they swayed and bounced around in the sky. He saw the first glow of dawn lighten the sky, heard the sounds of men stirring on deck and Fitzroy shaving and spluttering in the wash room, but neither the Captain's cheery greeting nor the fragrant smell of bacon could draw him from his bed. He lay moaning for the remainder of the morning, staggering to the wash room twice to retch violently on an empty stomach.

It must have been well into the afternoon when, drowsing uneasily, Darwin heard a timid knock on the cabin door. Not having the strength to answer nor the inclination to receive visitors, he turned over and buried his head in the pillow. Seconds later he felt a hand on his shoulder and turned to meet the familiar scowl of the stores' boy, Ben Sweet.

The boy held out a bowl of thin, colourless liquid, which, for all its tastelessness and Darwin's lack of appetite, actually stayed down and caused some small improvement in the invalid's spirits.

"That was thoughtful of you, lad," said Darwin, smiling weakly. "You owed me a good turn, though."

"It was orders," mumbled Sweet. "You ain't the only one seasick in his bunk." For a second the scowl might have passed for a mischievous grin.

"I daresay," replied Darwin, "on this pitching switchback of an ocean."

"We are scarcely out to sea yet," jeered the boy, "and it's only a light wind that's driving us. You'll see worse, but mebbee you'll have your sea legs afore then."

"Never," moaned Darwin, "I doubt I'll live that long."

The boy smiled, the first real smile Darwin had seen on his face. "Ah, you'll come through. Give it time."

"What's your name, lad," asked Darwin, "and how did you come by *your* sea legs?"

"'Tis Sweet, Ben Sweet, an' I was born to it. Me dad and his dad afore him, they were shipwrights. They built boats all their lives."

"Your father's dead then?" enquired Darwin gently.

"Ay." The dark scowl returned to Ben's face. "And like as not I'll be too if I don't get back." And grabbing the empty broth bowl, he fled.

By next morning Darwin's interest in the world was sufficiently restored for him to welcome Ben and his breakfast of hot sago, gently spiced and fragrant. As he ate, he sat quietly upon the chart locker watching the boy.

Ben seemed in no hurry to go. He idly touched the precious seafaring instruments that crammed the shelves and lockers of the small cabin. Finding several shallow trays of sand, his curiosity got the better of him.

"They contain chronometers," explained Darwin, "twenty-two of them, for Captain Fitzroy means to keep perfect time upon this ship. But let me show you the binnacle compasses, Ben, for they are instruments of equal accuracy and precision. See how finely the magnetised needles are balanced to hold their north pointing positions."

Ben was already familiar with the sextant and knew how to line up the position of the sun and that of the horizon in order to fix the ship's latitude at sea.

A growing appreciation of the boy's intelligence and talent led Darwin to show Ben his large library of books; the studies of well-known geologists, botanists and explorers, and the pincers, nets, jars, surgeon's knives, trays and other assorted paraphernalia which would help Darwin's own studies during the voyage. "It'll be a long trip then?" asked Ben.

"Several years," answered Darwin, "didn't you know?"

"It's of no matter to me," shrugged the boy, and slowly Darwin drew from him the sad account of his father's death, and how Captain Fitzroy, upon visiting the shipwright's yard, found only the orphaned son, alone and bitter. "He said I could come on board from respect for my father's work, and earn my keep by my labour, but he's never worked for that devil quartermaster hisself, now has he?"

"Nevertheless, it was a kind act," said Darwin sternly, "and one you must repay by your effort. You owe yourself something too, Ben. Don't let this adventure pass by as a suffrance on your part. I myself have vowed to use every second of this voyage to improve myself and my knowledge and you must do the same."

Maybe this sharp lecture worked, for when Darwin spread the finely detailed sea charts upon the table, Ben joined eagerly in tracing the line of their forthcoming journey, almost due south to the coast of BRAZIL, down the east coast of SOUTH AMERICA and up the west coast. From there they would cross the Pacific Ocean to the *Galapagos Islands,* to the islands of the South Pacific, NEW ZEALAND, AUSTRALIA and thence across the Indian Ocean to SOUTH AFRICA and home.

"So you see, Ben, you will grow from a boy to a young man on this ship, and for both of us this voyage may prove a turning point in our lives."

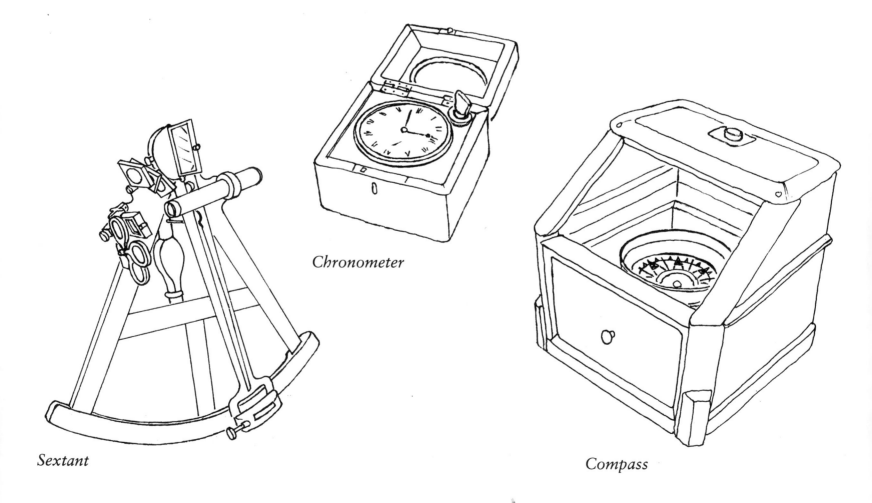

Sextant

Chronometer

Compass

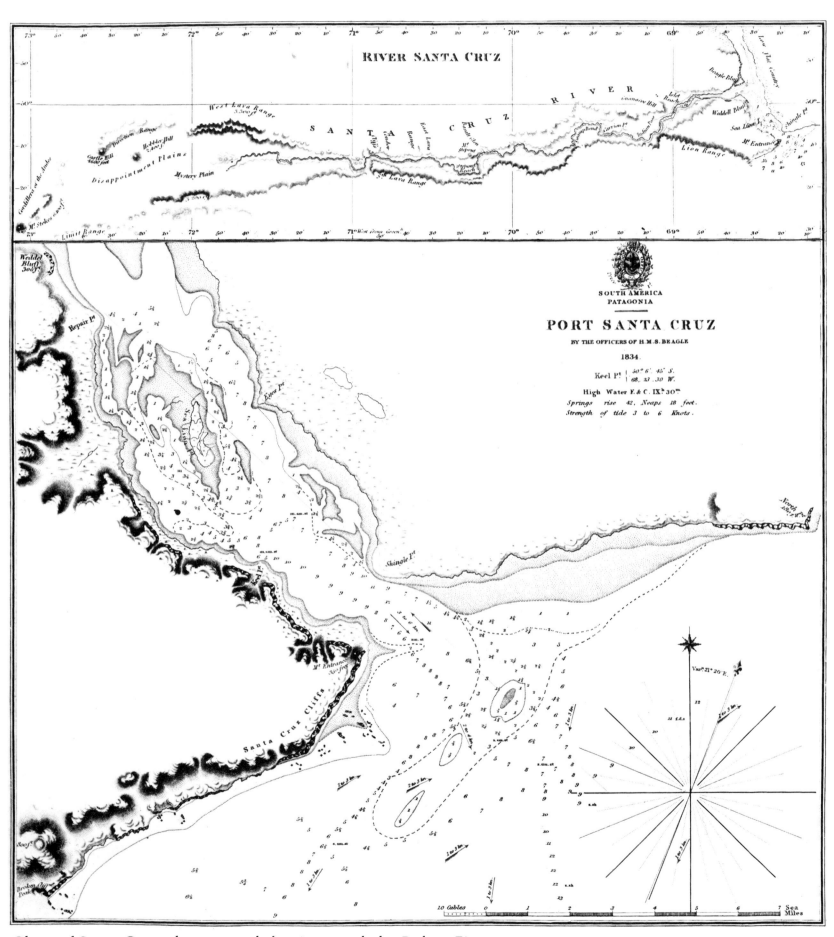

Chart of Santa Cruz, the port and the river, made by Robert Fitzroy and the officers of HMS Beagle during the voyage.

POOP
DECK

POOP
CABIN

HOLD situated under lower deck

HMS Beagle

In the midst of the avid discussion, Darwin was surprised to find he was feeling better and he suggested a turn on deck to get some fresh air.

"There are parts of this ship I have yet to see, Ben. Come, we will explore and you shall be my crutch and guide."

"The quartermaster'll see that I don't get far, Mr. Darwin," said the boy, shaking his head.

"I will speak to the Captain on your behalf, Ben. It occurs to me that the quartermaster has less need of your particular talents than I. Would you like to help me, by way of collecting my specimens and cataloguing, and doing some detailed sketchwork?"

"I would indeed," cried the boy, unable to suppress a grin which spread from ear to ear.

UPPER DECK
1 top gallant forecastle
1a patent windlass under forecastle
1b small cabin under forecastle
1c bowsprit under forecastle
2 foremast
3 galley ventilator and chimney
4 forehatch
5 cutter inside yawl
6 booms, spare spars
7 gangways
8 main hatch
9 main mast
10 main bits
11 gun room skylight
12 after companion
13 captain's skylight
14 cutter
15 captain's whaleboat
16 poop deck
 dots indicate poop cabin under
a table
b bookshelves
c Mr Darwin's storage chests
d chart locker
e Stokes's cabin
f steering wheel
g w.c.

17 mizzen mast
18 poop cabin skylight
19 azimuth compass
20 jolly boat
21 signal flag lockers
22 poop ladders
23 6 pounder guns
24 brass 9 pounder guns

LOWER DECK
1 sick bay and men's lockers
2 galley
3 men's bags
4 men's messes
5 midshipmen's chests
6 gun room steward
7 gun room store room
8 dispensary
9 captain's steward
10 store room
11 assistant surgeon
12 master's chaffers
13 1st Lt Wickham
14 boatswain's cabin
15 gunner's cabin
16 carpenter's cabin
17 midshipman's berth
18 Parson Rowlett
19 Surgeon Bynet
20 2nd Lt Sullivan
21 gun room
22 gun room table
23 buffet
24 passage
25 chronometer room
26 wash room
27 captain's cabin
28 table
29 Mr Darwin's seat at dinner
30 Captain Fitzroy's seat at dinner
31 Captain Fitzroy's writing desk
32 Captain Fitzroy's bed
33 sofa and bed
34 wash room
35 lockers
36 jolly boat

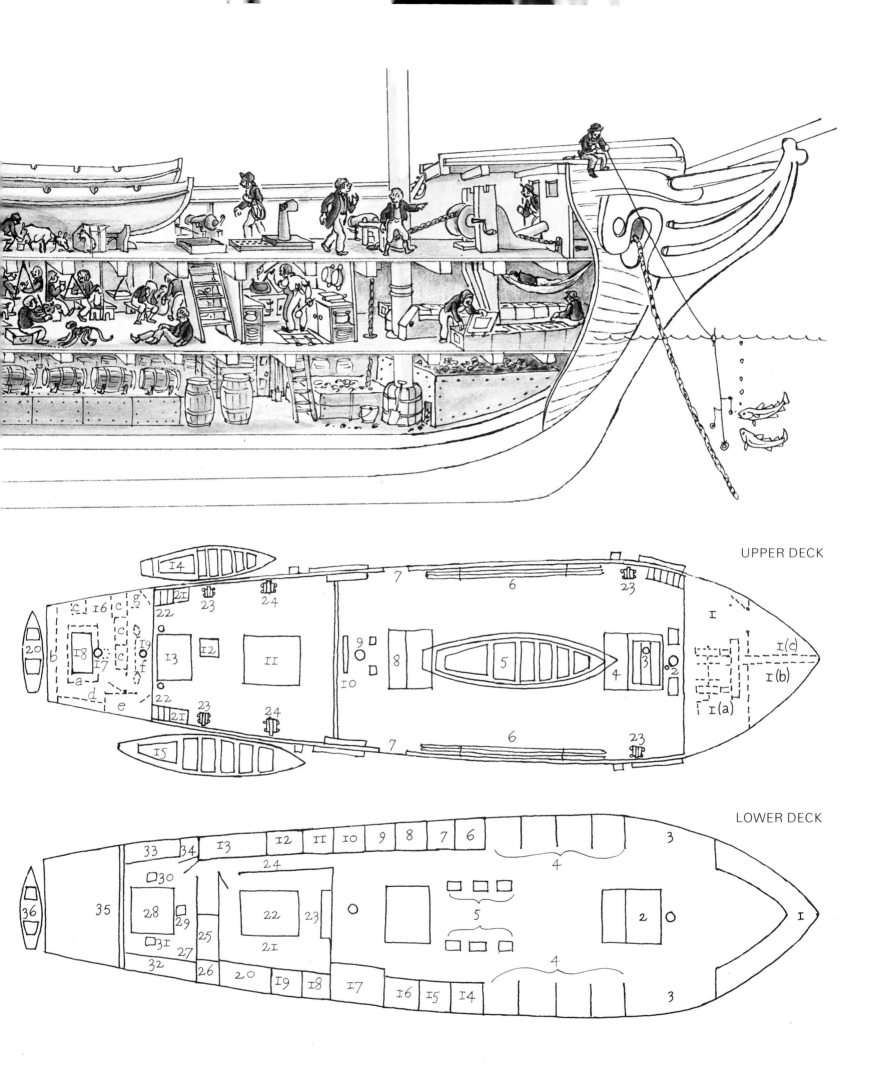

UPPER DECK

LOWER DECK

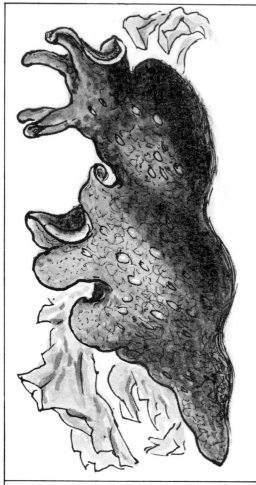

As predicted, Darwin's 'sea legs' grew steadier day by day, and he became restless to begin work as a naturalist. The disappointing news that the ship could not land at the island of *Tenerife* but must sail on for a further nine days to the islands of *Cape Verde,* led him to construct a kind of trawl net. The net, in the shape of a large bag held open at one end by a semi-circular bow, could be dragged along behind the ship.

Each haul contained a mass of tiny sea creatures, many of which Darwin had never seen before. Carefully he sorted them out on the deck, putting to one side those of most interest to be studied more closely in the poop cabin. Although most of these marine animals were very simple forms of life and only important insofar as they provided food for larger fish, seen under the microscope they took on exquisite shapes and colours.

But this was only the beginning. On 16th January 1832 they landed at *Cape Verde Islands* and having set up a base on *Quail Island,* Darwin and Ben set about exploring this seemingly desolate place. The island was only a kilometre or so in circumference and for the next two days the pair covered every part of it, gathering a great harvest of animals, corals and chunks of volcanic rock.

Searching among the rock pools, Ben learned what to expect from an Aplysia. "It's nothing but a great fat sea slug," he said in disgust, prodding the large dirty-yellow creature with one finger. "It's feeding on some seaweed here. It's got feelers and purple-coloured veins running through its body, see?" And then Ben let out a sudden yelp, drawing back his finger. The slug, protesting at this interruption to its meal, had secreted a stinging liquid. Seconds later it emitted a purple-red substance which quickly stained the water in the pool and helped it make its escape.

Darwin laughed. "That may teach you to respect this octopus here," he said, beckoning to another pool. At first Ben couldn't make out the shape.

"It isn't easy to find," he said, "it seems to change its colour to match the background. See, purple to greenish-yellow and back to grey."

"That's the creature's best form of defence, Ben," said Darwin, "but if an enemy does catch up with it, it will shoot a jet of water from a tube at the side of its head, or like your sea slug, it will stain the water with coloured ink to hide its traces."

There was plenty of time to observe all these small sea creatures for the Beagle was now making its long sea journey across the Atlantic. It was some weeks before Darwin and Ben saw land, but it was interesting that when they finally landed at *St Paul's Rocks* they were to come across animals who, unlike the octopus and the sea slug, had no form of defence at all. The thousands of terns and boobies that crowded the jagged crags of *St Paul's Rocks* were so unused to men that the crew of the Beagle were able to clamber ashore without disturbing them. They gathered eggs from the nests and killed some birds for the evening meal by simply knocking them on the head with a stone.

Meanwhile at sea, the men were hooking and pulling in large fish despite a continuous battle against several sharks who were determined to wrest the catch from the sailors before they could heave it aboard.

above: Aplysia,
one of the many kinds of sea slug
below: Octopus

Mr. Darwin had given me this fine sketchbook in which he bids me keep my impressions of this voyage, and tells me he may make use of my drawings, being no artist himself. I shall thus devote the first page to Mr. Darwin since he's gone to his cabin worn to a thread by the day's events.

It was dark last night when the sea lord, Neptune, hailed us and came aboard, and from that time on there was no sense nor reason aboard. Every man got ready for the ceremony of 'Crossing the Line', whereby Neptune might exact his tributes from we poor wretches who'd never crossed the Equator before.

At nine o-clock this morning, we thirty two 'griffins' were led below deck and shut there in the dark and heat until Neptune's constables came to get us one

H.M.S. Beagle as Mr Darwin and I remember her at anchor
in Murray Narrow, Beagle Channel.

by one. Firstly I was blindfolded and sat upon a tilting plank, then the 'barber' smothered my head with a frothy lather of soap, black pitch and paint, and set about shaving me with a length of curved iron bar. I thought it was good sport until that mean, grit-faced quartermaster rammed into my mouth some filthy concoction that I had to spit out, it burned so. Then the plank tipped up and shot me head over heels into a bath of water, where strong hands grasped me and ducked me several times!

When they took the blindfolds from my eyes, I must bow to Neptune seated on the deck, and to his goddess, Amphritite, and to all kinds of weird devils bespattered and bedaubed with flour and brightly coloured paints. Meanwhile others danced wildly around and helped the 'barber' in his messy work. Mr Darwin joined in the fun tho' he thought everyone quite mad; but he sat by the Captain afterwards and received a share of the splashes as the water and paint flew about.

It was the end of February before the Beagle reached SOUTH AMERICA and put in at *San Salvador* on the coast of BRAZIL in order to take on water and provisions. The town stood in a perfect setting. It perched high above the bay, a cluster of tall, white houses set amongst dense woods. In the foreground, tall masted men-of-war and trading vessels lay at anchor in the calm waters of the *Bay of all Saints.*

As ever, Darwin was keen to get on land. The past weeks had been devoted entirely to collecting sea animals and recently in the shallow seas around the coast of BRAZIL, he had had a chance to gather corals and seashells. One fish in particular had caught Darwin's attention. The bridled burrfish had such a flabby skin that it could puff itself into a sphere by taking in air and water. When fully blown out, the bulges on its back would stiffen into sharp, protective prickles. The burrfish could also defend itself by secreting a dark red stain or by using its sharp teeth to attack. One had even been known to make its escape from the stomach of a shark by biting a way out!

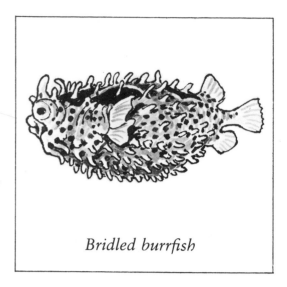

Bridled burrfish

However Darwin's real interest was in insects and for this he needed to explore the luscious vegetation of the Brazilian jungle.

The outskirts of the town of *San Salvador* pressed right against the dark wall of the rain forest, but here and there, in small hacked out clearings, a tangle of fruit and grain plants fought each other for survival. Darwin could only just stop Ben from abandoning the expedition in order to gorge himself on the bananas, oranges, pawpaws and other delicious fruits growing along the track.

"I'd like to be marooned *here*," said Ben munching into the flesh of a coconut he had cracked open to quench his thirst. "You could feast like a king on all this."

"I agree," said Darwin, pointing out corn; yams, that he said tasted like sweet potatoes; plantain, a kind of banana, and starchy cassava roots, "but we're not marooned yet, young Ben, and I fear I must tear you away from your meal if I am to make any headway with my exploration. At least I shall not be requiring you to work on an empty stomach!"

An hour's walk brought them into the thick of the forest. Darwin stood spellbound. Although the chorus of insect chirruping had almost deafened them along the path, here no sounds penetrated the absolute stillness. The trees pressed together, towering high above them like the masts of a ship, but so densely verdant that they shut out the sunlight. Where the branches did not touch lush bunches of Spanish moss, feathery liana creeper and large vivid flowers caught the filtered rays.

A bright eye gleamed from between the fronds of a cabbage palm, and a flash of bright feathers drew Ben's eye.

"Is it a parrot?" he whispered excitedly. "It's a toucan," replied Darwin, "another avid fruit eater like yourself. See the shape of the bill, there's your clue. Any bird whose main diet is fruit will have a wide, curved beak; a fish eater, on the other hand, must probe for his wriggling, slippery catch with a long, narrow bill. Insect

catchers have small pincer bills and nuteaters need a strong jaw. It's all detective work, you see, for those with sharp eyes."

There were several different kinds of humming-bird, all tiny, hovering around the flowers, and here and there chasing off a rival butterfly intent upon the nectar. Their wings moved so rapidly that they did not seem to be moving at all. Only the whirring hum and the rapid speed at which they were able to dart about, showed what efficient steering aids these busy wings really were.

Darwin and Ben had reached a particularly overgrown spot when rain started to fall in warm, heavy drops, thudding down through the glossy foliage and filling the air with steaming dampness. Surprised that the forest canopy should provide so little cover, they started back down the track at a run, but were thoroughly drenched before the downpour stopped as abruptly as it had started.

In the end Darwin was not disappointed for he was able to spend three whole months in BRAZIL, much of it in the village of *Botofogo* outside the capital, *Rio de Janeiro*. Here he rented a cottage from which it was easy to make regular visits into the rain forest. He never came back empty-handed.

Knowing that few species of the smaller tropical spiders and beetles had been seen in London, Darwin concentrated his efforts on collecting these. With Ben's help he was soon able to pack a large box of samples in cotton to send back to his old teacher and friend, Professor Henslow.

Ben soon learned what to look for, although the insects themselves went to great lengths to hide from him. It took a sharp pair of eyes to tell a dull-grey stick insect from a dull-grey piece of twig. It took experience to discover that an evil-looking scorpion was in fact a harmless moth, or that a poisonous fruit was really a beetle, both disguising themselves for protection against their predators. Darwin showed Ben a moth whose wings could have been mistaken for fallen leaves and another that resembled a cluster of flower petals.

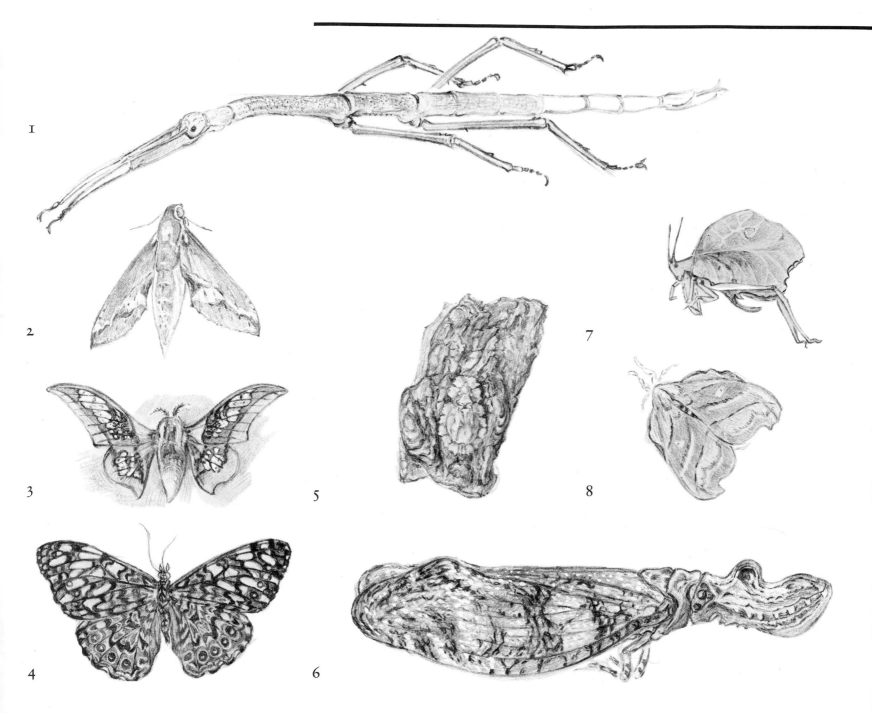

In the orange groves, Darwin collected several specimens of the grey-flecked Papilio Feronia, an unusual little butterfly which turned out to have a number of extraordinary tricks up its sleeve. From the beginning it was difficult to pick up with tweezers because of its habit of resting with outstretched wings and not folded ones like other butterflies. In addition it could use its legs to run away and several times shuffled out of Darwin's reach. He called Ben to listen to its loud clicking noise as it chased a female butterfly through the bushes, and even at a distance of twenty metres, the sound still reached them clearly.

Once they came across a fierce battle between a Pepsis wasp and a large spider. The wasp darted in to attack again and again and although the spider defended bravely, it was finally wounded, and crawled away into the long grass. The wasp did not give up. It hunted backwards and forwards, until, discovering the hideout of its prey, it dived in to deliver two sharp stings. As the spider lay dying, the wasp landed nearby to drag off the body.

"Ugh!" cried Ben, sweeping it away.

"Ugh, indeed!" echoed Darwin, flicking it off again. "Although the law of the jungle decrees that all living things must be hunter or hunted, my sympathies were definitely with the loser that time."

At night they would often sit outside the cottage listening to the chirruping chorus of cicadas, crickets and frogs, and watching the fireflies glittering in the hedgerows. Like the glow-worm, the insect's light came from a shiny fluid just below the surface of the skin. It shone clearly through two large rings on the insect's abdomen. When Darwin touched a firefly its lights would flash even more intensely and he noticed that these glowing patches continued to shine for almost twenty four hours after the insect was dead.

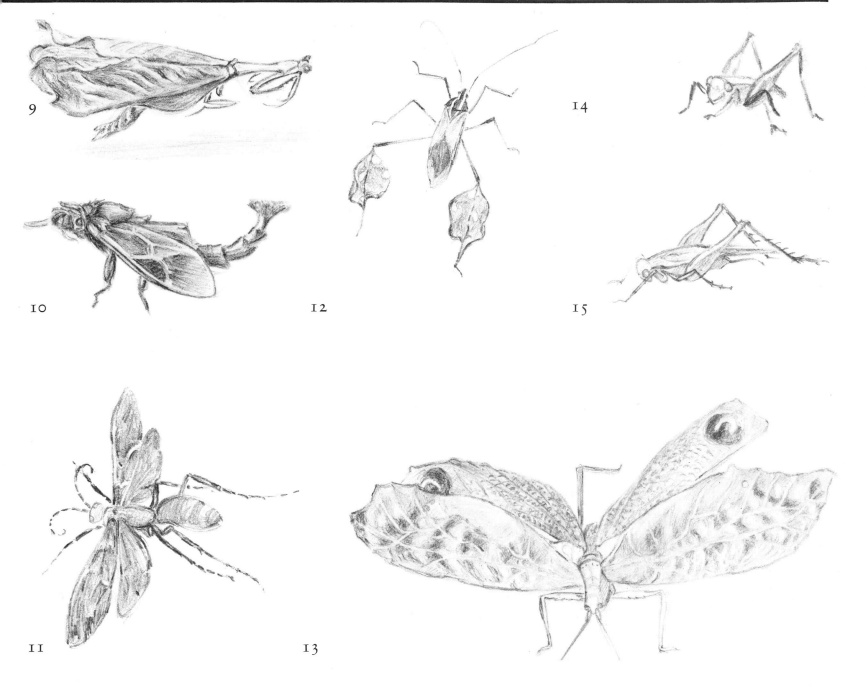

9

10

11

12

13

14

15

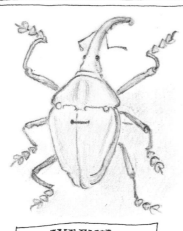

WEEVIL
Rhinastus Pertusus

WEEVIL
Cholus Imputatus

LONGHORN BEETLE
Coremia Hirtipes

DUNG BEETLE
Phanaeus Lucifer

STRAIGHT SNOUTED WEEVIL
Teramocerus Gracilis

LONGHORN BEETLE
Unxia Laeta

LEAF BEETLE
Doryphora Tessellata

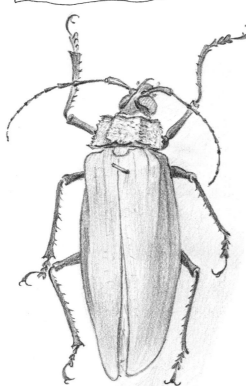

LONGHORN BEETLE
Ctenoscelis Acanthopus

ROVE BEETLE
Xantholinus Chalybeus

TORTOISE BEETLE
Selenis Nebulosa

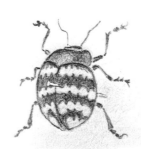

LEAF BEETLE
Doryphora Batesii

DARKLING BEETLE
Otocerus Serraticornis

On one occasion, Darwin and Ben came back with sixty-eight different species of one tiny beetle. Darwin was overjoyed with this success. Carefully selecting just one of every kind for his zoological records, Darwin killed the insects with poison.

"I can fairly say that is the best bit of beetle foraging I have ever done," he said happily, as he and Ben sorted the insects into rows according to their colour, sex and markings and pinned them in neat rows in his sample trays.

"You'd never guess there were so many sorts," said Ben, scrutinising one particular beetle between his tweezers.

"I suspect there are even more to find," said Darwin, "certainly many more species than in England. As a young lad of your age I'd often creep out after school and go for long walks over the hills just to catch a few beetles. Mind you, I think I was escaping the stern attentions of my father and the tiresome company of four sisters as much as anything."

"I never thought much of school neither," agreed Ben, "tho' I wasn't there long enough to learn much. If no one was watching, I used to run off to fish from the wharf."

"We seem to have been a bright pair of pupils! I had a passion for angling too, I remember, and later on, shooting; but right from the beginning I took most pleasure in collecting; seashells, birds' eggs, just one from each nest, mind you, and insects, especially beetles."

"There was huge beetles in the rotten planking on the old boats," remembered Ben.

"Yes," said Darwin, "that's where I found them. I'd go scooping up the rubbish from the barges that brought reeds down from the fenland. Or I'd scrape the moss off old trees in winter time. I got some rare specimens that way."

"Did you know what each one was, like you do now?"

Darwin laughed. "Oh no I don't. Many of these are as new to me as they are to you, and I daresay they'll puzzle the experts back home too. But no, in those days I was just a collector, I never dissected them or took much trouble classifying them."

"There's so many here. Do we have space for them all?"

"There are more trays in the lockers." Darwin paused and a smile spread over his face. "I remember once when I did run out of space, at least I ran out of arms. I'd found a couple of beetles, both rare specimens, when I came upon a third and not wanting to lose it, I popped one of the first two into my mouth, whereupon it spurted out such a bitter tasting liquid that I was forced to spit it out."

"So you lost it," laughed Ben.

"I did, and the third one too."

Ben thought for a while. "You must be a very great man, Mr. Darwin, to be here on the Beagle with Cap'n Fitzroy. You must be very well-known for your collecting."

"Not at all, Ben. I am scarcely known at all as a naturalist. Indeed, my father would say I had a greater reputation as a failed doctor or a failed clergyman, since I completed my training in neither vocation. No, I regret I am quite a novice at this work, but I do have some good friends, like Professor Henslow whom I have mentioned before. It was he who recommended me to Captain Fitzroy and it is out of gratitude to him that I am determined to succeed with my discoveries."

"Then for my part," added Ben, "I am grateful to him too, for I am having an excellent time assisting you." He smiled at Darwin and turned back to the beetles. "See, this is my favourite one. Come on, you great ugly brute, I'll sketch you in my book as a memento of our day's hunting."

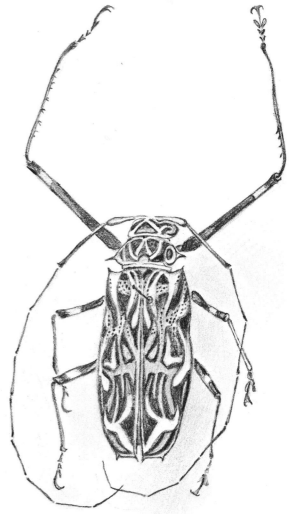

HARLEQUIN BEETLE
Acrocinus Longimanus

8th April 1832

On 8th April, Darwin and Ben were up early for Patrick Lennon, a local merchant in *Rio*, had promised to include them in a party visiting his large coffee estate some hundred miles inland. The party travelled on horseback, often through such dense jungle that a path had to be hacked through the ferns and bamboos. And in these wild, unexplored regions it seemed that small eyes watched their slow progress from the protective cover of the foliage, the eyes of a large Bearded Monkey, or a sloth. Sometimes they heard the howl of a jaguar or came upon a muddy lake where dozing alligators basked like innocent logs.

As they approached Lennon's hacienda they heard the echoing boom of a cannon and a bell began to toll. The master was returning and the slaves were summoned to greet him from the plantations. The manager welcomed Lennon and his guests and escorted them through an open yard bordered by stables, store rooms and the slaves' quarters and brought them to a thatched house with cool, white-washed walls and paneless windows. From the interior, Darwin watched the bustle of farm animals in the yard; dogs, hens, horses and pigs. It all seemed very picturesque as the women gathered round their cooking fires and naked children played in the sun. And

later that evening when the workers returned, they stood together under the stars and sang a hymn and Lennon read a prayer to bless the day's labour.

But Darwin had listened to his uncle Josiah Wedgwood speak out with great anger and feeling against the ills of slavery, and he shared the opinion that it was abominable for one man to own another. He was soon to see the cruelty that lurked behind the outward show of happy community life, for next morning, and for no apparent reason, Lennon flew into a violent temper and threatened to sell off the women slaves and all the children at the public auction in *Rio*. It was difficult for Darwin to keep his temper at the suggestion that so many closely united families should be broken up at the whim of one man. However, the plantation manager felt no restraint and he sprang to his feet angrily and drew a pistol at Lennon until Darwin and the other guests intervened.

This quarrel was soon forgotten but throughout his stay in BRAZIL Darwin saw many examples of cruelty to slaves and he longed for the day to come when slavery would be abolished and all men recognised as free.

Often on their forays into the jungle Darwin and Ben would come across lines of leaf-cutter ants scurrying backwards and forwards. They worked tirelessly as they cut the leaves with their powerful jaws and bore away large sections to the anthill. There the leaves would be worked into a rich mould compost in which fungus soon sprouted to provide food for the colony.

"Hundreds of thousands of ants live inside a vast network of tunnels and chambers," Darwin told Ben. "A fertile queen ant lays all the eggs while the infertile female ants act as soldiers or workers protecting the eggs and feeding the young larvae.

Ben watched the pattern of continuous movement along well-beaten paths for some time.

"Is that all they do all day?" he asked.

"That's how a large colony works best," Darwin answered. "Social animals like ants, rely upon each individual having a specific job to do and doing it to the best of its ability."

"Like the crew of the Beagle," said Ben smartly, remembering how the small ship had put on an impressive display of seamanship manoeuvring deftly under full sail into one port or another and often earning the praise and envy of less disciplined or well trained crews.

Leafcutter ants collecting pieces of leaf to nourish the fungi they grow for food on their nests.

Not half a mile from the anthill, they came upon a far more ferocious and disciplined swarm. Excitedly Darwin beckoned Ben over to a small, bare clearing where he had observed several spiders, cockroaches, lizards and other small animals rushing to and fro as if in great danger. And indeed they were. As they stared harder, it seemed that every leaf and stalk around the clearing was black with ants.

"Take care, Ben, come round this side." Darwin steered him into the undergrowth. "If I'm not mistaken, this is a swarm of nomadic army ants on the move and they are just about to encircle their prey on two flanks."

The advance of the army ants was relentless and they literally devoured everything in their path.

Leaving the battlefield that had evolved, Darwin and Ben followed the dense mass of the ant column back into the forest. It stretched almost a hundred metres and, here and there, Darwin was able to find places where ants had linked together to form living bridges, and in one or two cases, a round tube-like nest a metre across where the queen and her attendant nurses would have bivouaced previously.

"Where are they off to now?" asked Ben as finally they reached the tail of the column.

"To a fresh feeding ground where there are leaves and insects in plenty. Then they will once again form a living shelter for two or three weeks while foraging parties raid the jungle each day."

"They're so small and yet they're terrifyingly powerful," said Ben thoughtfully.

"They have strong instincts, that's all. They move and work fearlessly. They never deviate from the set path. If human beings didn't have the capacity to reason things out for themselves they might just have turned out the same."

It was now early July and the Beagle set sail on its southward journey through warm, blue, tropical seas. Darwin's second bad bout of sea sickness was almost as long lasting as the first, but this time Ben acted as his ears and eyes, bringing him regular bulletins about the activity on deck and at sea. When Darwin was too ill to stagger on deck, Ben would take his notebook to his favourite position astride the yard arm, and in this way nothing went unnoticed, not the spouting whales, nor the flying fish that sometimes leapt so high they flapped upon the deck, nor the hundreds of leaping porpoises who followed the ship for miles as it ploughed its course through the sea under full canvas. Even at a speed of nine knots the porpoises crossed and re-crossed sportingly in front of the bows, jumping clear out of the water before swerving away to the side of the ship. At night, beneath a sky lit by tropical storms, the sea glowed with phosphorescence and penguins left luminous tracks through the waves. And when they could not be seen, these barking or jackass penguins could be heard bellowing like cattle all round the ship.

Compared to the tranquility of the three months spent at work in the rain forests of BRAZIL, Darwin's first visit to URUGUAY proved to be a noisy, hostile affair. The first hint of rebellion in the country came when the Beagle sailed peacefully into *Montevideo Bay* to find a British fighting frigate already moored there. There had been some trouble in the town and the frigate's deck bristled with guns, cannons and fighting men, ready to leap into action should the British residents need any help. With a rebellion brewing, Darwin had to abandon any hope of studying the flora and fauna of the grassy plains that stretched invitingly as far as the eye could see.

· Captain Fitzroy was reassuring. "I have it on the best authority," he laughed, "that there have been at least fourteen separate rebellions recorded in these parts in the space of one year. We'll sail up the River Plate to *Buenos Aires,* the capital of ARGENTINA, and return here when things get quieter."

But a nasty surprise greeted them in *Buenos Aires* harbour for a blank shot, followed by a live round, came whistling over the bows and sent the crew scurrying into a state of readiness for battle action.

Threatening all kinds of vengeance on the city and its ill-mannered guardships, Fitzroy set sail again on the return trip to *Montevideo,* where they found the rebellion in full swing. The local head of police came aboard and begged Fitzroy's immediate help.

"A party of rebel soldiers have stormed the prison and released all the inmates, having first armed them and enlisted their help. It's a dangerous situation, sir, for they're a mutinous band of desperadoes. They've now captured the citadel and barricaded themselves in. Frankly they'd be no threat to us at all if the town's entire store of ammunition wasn't kept there."

"I don't want the Beagle getting mixed up in these local quarrels," said Fitzroy severely, "but if, as you say, the lives and property of British citizens may be threatened, then my crew is at your service."

Everyone was delighted with the news of this unexpected call to arms. After several weeks at sea and the frustration of not being able to land at two different ports, the possibility of taking on a wild band of armed rebels sent the blood racing.

Darwin's reaction was no different. Thrusting two pistols into his belt and seizing a cutlass, he swung down the boarding netting and joined the crew in the whale boat.

But the night proved disappointingly uneventful. Gathered in the central fort, the fifty two men from the Beagle kept watch over the surrounding districts, where, it was rumoured, the rebels had

planted arms among their sympathisers. But the town seemed deserted and soon the crew drew out their cards and settled down to enjoy a meal of thick beefsteaks. By morning, government reinforcements had arrived in the town and had soon overthrown the rebel stronghold without a drop of blood being spilled.

Ben was highly dismayed. He had spent the entire night mastering the use of his cutlass and he was eager for a little cut and thrust action to test his newfound skills.

"It's my belief we should stay," he grumbled. "We are worth ten of each of these Uruguayans and like as not they'll need our help before the day's out." Nor was he any happier when he arrived back at the ship to discover that all the real excitement of the night had taken place there. "We could 'ear them blackguards lurking round the boat through the darkness," one of the ship's boys confided, "but tho' we shone the lamps out to sea, they kept themselves hidden. So guards were set on the ammunition store and we spiked the

guns ready for action should they dare to steal aboard. It was right shivery, I can tell 'ee, peering into that pitch blackness, 'earing nothing but the dip o' their paddles." "Never mind, Ben." Darwin patted his shoulder. "We'll find you some excitement yet. Let's go and sort those black-veined beetles we brought in from the swamp."
"Beetles!" snorted Ben.

7th September 1832

On 7th September 1832, the Beagle sailed a few hundred miles south to the small town of *Bahia Blanca*. This was to be the base from which the Beagle and its survey boats would make frequent trips to map the coastline of PATAGONIA. Here, too, Darwin was about to make one of his most exciting discoveries.

"It doesn't look much," said Ben in dismay as he surveyed the endless expanse of bleak mud-flats and reed-choked shallows that stretched away to the treeless desert plains beyond.

"We'll put in there," Darwin pointed to a bank some six metres higher than other parts of the shoreline where the cliff had been carved away by the sea to reveal layers of shingle and clay.

The beach below the cliff was gravelly. Ben kicked a pebble here and there; turned a small boulder, trickled sand through his fingers.

"Found any good shells?" he called over his shoulder.

"No," came the steady reply, "but what would you say to a fossilised tooth?"

It was indeed. A blunted molar from some very, very large animal. They fell to with a will, hacking away at the soft rock and shifting the shingle. After a few hours they had an amazing collection of bones and other fossils to show for their efforts.

"Is it all one animal?" asked Ben, holding up a gigantic tusk and claw.

"No, I think we've unearthed at least three different creatures here," replied

Darwin, scrutinising the skull and section of scaly, protective shell lying at his feet. "One thing I can say, these animals have been extinct for millions of years and we shall be fortunate if we get any zoological help in identifying all of them for I believe some are quite unknown."

It was growing dark but Darwin was too enthralled to return to the ship. He and Ben set up a makeshift camp on the beach and vowed to make an early start with their hammers and pickaxes.

By the end of the next day the jigsaw puzzle was almost complete.

"Now these claws almost certainly belong here," said Darwin piecing together a final skeleton, "making this a megatherium, a giant ground sloth that must have lived about two million years ago at a time we now call the Pleistocene period."

"Was it a fierce hunter?" asked Ben viewing the sharp claws doubtfully.

"Oddly no. It was a plant eater and those claws were used to hook down branches from the tree-tops."

When the boat returned to collect them, the sailors stared in mock dismay at the heap of dry, dusty bones to be conveyed aboard the Beagle, but Darwin ignored the jokes and laughter and insisted that every last tooth be carefully handled.

Megatherium

Hippidion

Fossil bones of the Megatherium, Hippidion, Toxodon and Macrauchenia, some of the South American mammals that Darwin found on his travels. All these mammals were extinct by the end of the Pleistocene, about 2 million years ago.

Megatherium was the largest of the giant ground sloths, and exceeded an elephant in size. It had huge claws and walked on the side of it's feet. It probably browsed on trees, or dug up roots.

Hippidion was a primitive horse that once roamed the plains of South America in large herds. When the other animals became extinct, it too died out,

Macrauchenia

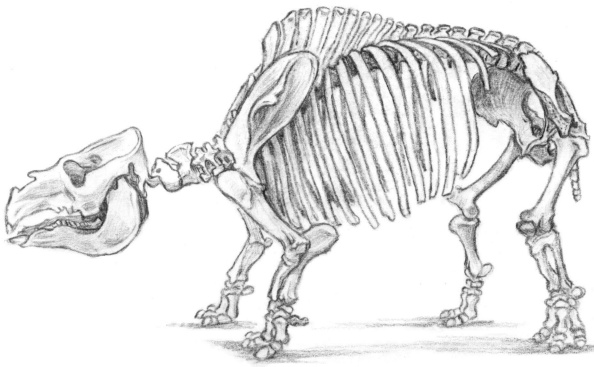

Toxodon

for it bears no relation to the modern horse, introduced to this continent in the sixteenth century by the Spaniards.

The Toxodon *was the largest and one of the latest of the notoungulates, which were unique to South America. Built rather like a rhinoceros, it probably* browsed on roots and weeds in shallow waters, as well as on dry land.

The Macrauchenia *was a large camel-type animal with a long neck. It was a plant eating mammal and may have been giraffe-like in habit.*

As the months passed and the Beagle made repeated visits to *Bahia Blanca*, Darwin's collection of bones grew, and complete skeletons began to take shape. Soon the time came to number and label the parts and crate them for their homeward journey to England.

Ben stared at the assortment of bones arranged upon the ground. "It's hard to think the likes of these are gone for ever." He frowned with disappointment. "They're truly what you told me then, extinct?"

"These particular giants are no more," confirmed Darwin, "but their descendants do still exist, albeit in smaller similar looking species. What puzzles me is that these giants were still living here until two million years ago, that's quite recent by geological reckoning, and one wonders what occurred then to destroy the thousands of monsters that swarmed this continent."

Ben put his mind to the problem. "Perhaps there was a drought," he suggested, "and their food supply was ruined and they all starved, or," his eyes lit up, "maybe there was a great flood that drowned them all." As this earned no response, he tried again. "Maybe the other animals killed them, ate the weakest, the young 'uns, so they all died out in time. Or maybe it was man who hunted them because he liked roasted armadillo or whatever, or drove them off so he could fence in the land for his own use."

Although Ben had thought Darwin was paying no attention he had been listening intently.

Extinct and living Edentates of South America. Glyptodon from the Pleistocene period. (Family Glyptodontidae)

"Well done, Ben. I'm quite certain that many species did become extinct and still are becoming so for one or more of the reasons you've mentioned. However, I think there was one other factor in this case, a very important one. It's my belief that SOUTH AMERICA was once an island and not joined to NORTH AMERICA by the isthmus of *Panama* at all. I believe these large, clumsy animals evolved here untroubled by problems of climate, food or predators for many millions of years.

Then, as the land bridge of CENTRAL AMERICA formed to connect the two continents, all kinds of strong predators moved southwards and these monster animals were too defenceless, too clumsy and too slow to escape their fate."

"But not all the large animals died out," reasoned Ben, "for there are still giant armadillos, tho' they're half the size that these must have been."

"I confess I have a theory about that too," said Darwin, "although it is only half formed in my mind and lacks a great deal of evidence. The armadillo we see now is smaller so it needs less food. It has possibly a more varied diet so it doesn't rely on supplies of just one kind of food. Undoubtedly it can move faster, dig a deeper burrow or curl into a tighter ball when pursued. All these changes won't have happened overnight, you understand, but very, very gradually from one generation to another, so that today we have a species of armadillo that is just better suited to survive."

Giant armadillo. (Family Dasypodidae)

As the Beagle's work took the ship increasingly southwards, Captain Fitzroy set a date for a visit to *Tierra del Fuego*, a bleak, bitterly cold and seldom visited island at the tip of SOUTH AMERICA. The Captain, alone, looked forward to the visit with great excitement, for he was about to conclude one of the most valuable experiments in the history of Christianity, or so he believed.

This was Captain Fitzroy's second visit to these parts. On his previous voyage some three years before, he had taken aboard some Fuegian natives and transported them to England for the sole purpose of educating them in civilised ways and in the Christian faith, then returning them to their own people. It had been a mammoth task, the size of which Darwin did not appreciate until he met Fuegians in their own primitive, if not barbaric state. Aboard the Beagle he passed cheerful times with Jemmy Button, and had more than once tried to question the moody York Minster and the shy little Fuegia Basket about their homeland, but they showed slight interest in drawing comparisons about their past and present lives.

Richard Matthews, the young and rather inexperienced missionary who hoped to land with the three homecomers and build a missionary station, also seemed somewhat unclear about what he was taking on. He was cheerfully optimistic, like the Captain, that there would be few problems in establishing an outpost of Christianity in this far-flung spot.

If anything, Ben had gleaned the most information. When there were shell samples to wash or animal skins to clean and stretch, he and Jemmy could often be seen squatting together in some corner of the deck, chatting away is if they had known each other for years.

The Beagle's arrival in TIERRA DEL FUEGO in November 1832 was indeed a bleak one, for mountainous seas threatened to engulf the ship more than once and the rugged, barren rocks along the coast seemed less than hospitable. It was sharp-eyed Jemmy who first caught sight of several of his countrymen concealed among the trees that shaded an overhanging rock. No threats being indicated from either side, the Beagle dropped anchor and the crew took in the sail while the Fuegians leaped up and down in greeting, uttering strange wild cries and waving their tattered cloaks. Throughout the night their camp fires burned along the cliffs, lending reality to the name TIERRA DEL FUEGO, Land of Fire.

The next morning, Fitzroy decided to send a small landing party to greet the natives, and for the first time Darwin was able to judge the primitive state of these islanders. Although he was to meet other members of other tribes, he found that the basic qualities of Fuegian life and behaviour varied little.

Most were tall, well-built people though their bodies were often deformed and bent from crouching in their fishing canoes or low, skin huts. They grew their hair long and left it matted and filthy, although they paid great attention to their copper-skinned faces, painting them with red and black stripes and drawing white circles round the eyes. They shaved roughly with sharp shells and coated their bodies with thick layers of grease as protection against the icy winds and stinging sleet and rain. Their clothing consisted either of a short cloak of guanoco skin, or, more often, of nothing at all. It was not difficult to understand how Fuegia and Jemmy had grasped their dainty manners with such ease, for the Fuegians proved excellent mimics. Their own language was formed by a series of low, throaty sounds and grunts, but they used facial expressions, hands and contorted bodies to convey messages to the party of white-skinned strangers.

Jemmy is my friend. He is sixteen so he is older than me, but being short for his age we stand about the same height. I often sketch Jemmy for he is a little vain and likes to pose for my drawings. If I get some feature wrong to his mind, he will rush off in a fury and return with his looking glass, which he pushes before me pointing wildly at my error, as if to show the reflection does not lie as I do. He is for ever polishing his boots upon which there must be not one speck of dust and he wears his white kid gloves at every opportunity although they run the risk of gathering dirt and tar as do all things at sea. I scarcely dare tease him tho' he teases me. He is a cheerful mimic, sharp-eyed and quick-witted and often has all on board laughing at his antics. Jemmy looks forward to going home for he means to show off his new ways to his family, those same natives who sold him to the Captain for the price of one pearl button. He says his country is good and so are his people, but I think he has forgotten many details for he was only a young boy when he left, and when I question him closely, he looks shy and shakes his head.

Fuegia is very nice. She is always kind and helpful towards Mr. Darwin and me, although I think, quite shy and modest. She learned very civilised ways in England and her dress is always neat and pretty as becomes a young lady who met the King and Queen of England. Fuegia picks up things very quickly for she understands our English language and speaks some Spanish and Portuguese learned during the past year's travels.

This is York Minster. He is a short man but his body is thick and powerful and as strong as that of any Jack Tar. Once I saw him lose his temper very passionately with my old enemy, the quartermaster, and I swear he might have done him violent damage had others not come between them. He is grown very fond of Fuegia Basket, although he says nothing outright, but they tease him on board, calling her his sweetheart, at which he grows moody and quiet. He does not like such teasing nor the way the sailors look at her and throw her pretty compliments.

45

In a quiet, pretty inlet named *Woolya Cove,* the ship's company set about unloading Matthew's tents and equipment and the various assortment of gifts and personal possessions brought from England by the three Fuegians. The entire crew set to with a will to erect a makeshift camp and to dig and plant out a small garden. While they worked, the local natives gathered round curiously to watch, until a crowd of at least a hundred had formed.

Among them were Jemmy's family who were quite overwhelmed by their grand relation. The women ran and hid and were too frightened to greet him but his four brothers walked round and round, viewing him in a very suspicious manner, until Jemmy cried out a greeting, forgetting that they could understand no English, and revealing, for the first time, that he had entirely forgotten his own language.

Darwin watched all this with a growing sense of unease. The gap between the two groups of people on the beach was far too wide for Fitzroy's experiment to work. The Fuegian natives were virtually nomadic and would not gather under the shelter of a missionary settlement. They

did not cultivate the soil nor did they build a stable home. They were aggressive and cruel to their children and continually at war with neighbouring tribes. Indeed, they were cannibals and when food went short, would eat their old women in preference to their dogs, whom they considered more useful. Darwin doubted whether Jemmy and the others had received sufficient teaching in the scriptures to be of much use to Matthews in spreading Christianity, or whether their own people would so much as listen to them anyway.

He was soon to be proved right. Having left the group to their own devices for ten days, the Beagle returned to *Woolya* to find that Matthews had been robbed of everything, threatened and beaten. Jemmy had tried to help but York Minster and Fuegia had sided with their own people. Nothing remained but the trampled ruins of the camp and garden. Matthews returned to the ship in a state of shock. Fitzroy too was bewildered. They had wanted so much to help and could not understand how much harm they had done by interfering with the course of nature, by trying to change the natives' own established, if primitive, way of life and not allowing them to make the gradual adjustment to civilisation on their own.

With some relief the crew of the Beagle returned to its work on the coastline of PATAGONIA and Darwin sought an excuse to escape the ship and Fitzroy's perpetual brooding at the failure of the Fuegian mission. Rather recklessly he decided to set off on an eight hundred mile trek overland from *El Carmen* to *Santa Fe*, stopping briefly at *Bahia Blanca* to check in with the Beagle, and again at *Buenos Aires*. He wanted to be quite free to observe the country, but was eventually persuaded to allow a group of local men to accompany him. The Argentinians and Indian tribes were waging a fierce war throughout the plains, fighting for possession of the land. The Indians were struggling to keep their independence; the freedom to roam at will hunting the rhea for its meat and feathers, while, the Argentinians wanted to fence off the land for their cattle.

Darwin's bodyguard consisted of a guide and six gauchos, the wild, tough cowboys of the Pampas. Proud and temperamental, they grew long moustaches and wore scarlet ponchos over wide trousers and tall, spurred white boots. They were superb horsemen, riders at one with their horses which they drove at breakneck speed over rough ground, across wide, fast flowing rivers, through desert and mountain alike.

Ben was allowed to make the first part of the journey. He soon grew to love those dare-devil horsemen as much as Darwin and began to copy their style of riding and hunting with reasonable success. With a knife tucked in his belt and a bola in his right hand, he would urge his horse forward to the chase, whirling the weapon wildly round his head as he galloped. The idea was to keep hold of the smallest of the three stones on the end of its thong, while spinning the other two round to gather speed. Once released, the whole missile caught the animal's hind legs with such revolving force, that the beast became entangled and was brought to the ground. Often the gauchos would gallop off in all directions as if on some vast orbit only to reappear in a great circle driving their hunted prey before them. It was an easy task to catch the animals with bolas once they were confined in a central spot.

At the end of the day the gauchos would light a fire of bones over which to roast meat, sing haunting songs on the guitar, brew their maté, and more often than not, end up brawling and very drunk.

At this point Darwin and Ben would discreetly withdraw, spread their blankets beside the camp fire and soon fall asleep under the stars.

Flamingo   *Rhea*

Hog nosed skunk

The pampas of ARGENTINA proved a very inhospitable region. The grassy plains of the coastal areas soon gave way to desert spotted with thorny bushes and dry scrub. However, despite the shortage of vegetation and water, there was a surprising number of different animals to enjoy.

The guanaco travelled in herds of between fifty and five hundred head. It was watchful and shy, aware that its enemies were powerful and wily. A fully-grown guanaco was seldom cornered. It could race as fast as any horse and put on such a display of fierce neighing, stamping and rearing as to make any hunter watchful.

The rhea was a smaller species of ostrich. Although unable to fly, it could achieve great speeds on its long legs by spreading its wings to the wind, and even without webbed feet, was a powerful swimmer. On his travels, Darwin learned of a new species of rhea, a rare kind with dark mottled feathers, scaled legs and feathers below its knees. This new discovery was later named Rhea Darwinii.

The giant armadillo was protected by armour of large bone plates joined together with skin. It ate insects and other small animals and was in turn hunted by man for its tasty flesh. When pursued the armadillo would burrow to safety in the dusty soil and was gone in a flash.

The vizcacha, Patagonian cavy and capybara were all rodents. The vizcacha dug a vast tunnel network underground, stripping the ground around the tunnel entrance to afford a clear view of approaching danger. It shared its tunnel with the burrowing owl, often to be seen on sentinel duty at the entrance. The capybara lived above ground in large colonies of several hundred animals. It looked like a large guinea pig but was more closely related to the water rat in its habits. When danger approached it would dive quickly into the water and swim powerfully away.

Vizcacha

Burrowing owl

Patagonian cavy

Black necked swan

Capybara

13th April 1834

On the 13th April 1834, the Beagle put in at the mouth of the *Santa Cruz River* and beached for repairs. After almost two years charting the eastern coastline of SOUTH AMERICA the crew had believed themselves well underway for the western coast, but the ship had scraped its keel on a rock and had now to be repaired before the voyage could continue.

Recognising that most of the crew would be sitting around idly for the next few days Captain Fitzroy suggested that they pass the time in exploring.

"Let's take three boats up river and try and reach the Andes mountains," he said to Darwin. "From all accounts no one has set foot in the interior before and we should find plenty of wild life thereabouts." So next day three whale boats were piled with provisions and the party set off upstream.

At first the going was easy. A good wind and a fast tide carried them past low, flat-topped banks of shingle and mud, behind which the desert plains stretched far into the distance.

"There isn't a lot going on in these parts," muttered Ben, "'cept a lot of mud banks and a fair pile of sand."

"Nothing much going on indeed!" retorted Darwin. "Then what do you think those dark-coloured animals are, crossing the stream ahead?" But before Ben could answer, the question was answered, for the bobbing figures reached the bank and started to clamber ashore on stilt-like legs.

"Rhea," exclaimed Fitzroy, as they watched the birds shaking water from their feathers. "I had no idea they could

swim." A few yards further on they spotted a large herd of guanoco, some five thousand strong, standing quite still and alert on the lava plain.

"And tonight, young man," said Fitzroy, "you shall help stand watch over the camp in case of an Indian attack. That will teach you to keep your eyes open."

The river was tidal for some distance but soon the current turned against them and the wind died down. The only way to go on was by hauling the boats. Each man took up a long rope with a collar fixed to one end and bent his back to the task. It was heavy, tiring work, especially when rapids churned the river shallows, or the banks rose to jagged ravines and the pullers had constantly to cross from one side of the river to the other in order to gain a foothold.

Frequently Darwin and Ben went on ahead to reconnoitre and hunt game. Soon they had a wonderful view of the high mass of the *Andes* range, capped with a shining white snow and crested with cloud. They had come two hundred and forty five miles inland and now everyone worked with a will to reach the foothills of the mountains. Darwin longed to start work examining their geological formation.

But rations were running low and Fitzroy became anxious to return to the ship. Darwin had to be content with the knowledge that in under two months he would be sailing on the far side of that insuperable range, and then he would get his chance to explore.

In icy winds and heaving seas they set
sail for the Pacific. There was no need
to round the tip of *Cape Horn* for a deep
channel known as the *Magellan Strait*
carved a short cut through the islands
north of TIERRA DEL FUEGO.

Immediately upon entering the channel, the Beagle was dwarfed by high
mountain cliffs, icy glaciers and pre-
cipices that rose on either side. Here and
there thundering cascades crashed from a
great height into the sea, sending up a
blinding spray of icy mist.

All was blue and sea green, steel grey
and dazzling white, the silent chill colours
of perpetual winter, only softened each
evening by the warm glint of the setting
sun.

On one such evening a party landed.
They hauled up their boats and camped
on the beach for the evening meal. Suddenly a large chunk of the ice cliff broke
away, followed by a landslide of shifting
snow. The canyons and valleys echoed to
the rumble of the moving mass, and the
sea rose up in great rollers and surged in
over the beach.

The party scrambled for protection or
flung themselves over the boats and provisions to prevent them being dragged
away. Fresh waves swept them down the
beach and again and again the men had to
struggle to the ropes to haul them back.

From then on, the journey continued
with fresh vigour for everyone was
keen to reach the open sea.

Even so it took a month to break
through. The channel was perilously narrow in parts due to icebergs and if the
Beagle strayed too near the cliffs it was
liable to be hit by great chunks of falling
ice. Snow covered the decks and ice
formed on the rigging. The men began to
grumble, they felt ill; their wet clothes
never had time to dry out; the food was
terrible.

22nd July 1834

Fossils found by Darwin in various parts of South America. Tertiary era.

Fusus subreflexus

Fusus pyruliformis

So, when on 22nd July 1834, the Beagle finally reached the smart, well-ordered Chilean capital of *Valparaiso* with all its home comforts, good food and sunny weather, everyone's spirits soared. Darwin had a single purpose.

"Come on, Ben," he urged, "we must find guides and mules and get ourselves up into those mountains."

Climbing in the *Andes* was unbelievable. The mules picked their way up narrow stony tracks, along overhanging ledges and over craggy peaks. The air was dry and clear and the view extended for miles. Each day they journeyed higher, camping out at night round the fire.

From every viewpoint the mountain chain could be seen as a massive backbone to the South American continent. Darwin grew increasingly curious as to how it had been formed. This time it was Ben's sharp eyesight that unearthed the first clue. He held the perfectly formed fossilised sea shell between his fingers and peered at it.

"What is this doing up here," he muttered, "and see here, another one?" He gazed around. "A whole bed of them just like you get down on the sea-shore."

Darwin took the fossils from Ben and lapsed into deep thought. He showed little surprise either, when, lower down the mountain side they came upon a small forest of chalky-white petrified trees.

Then he spoke. "Just as I thought! I am now almost sure that these mountains used to be under the ocean."

"They what?" said Ben incredulously.

"And these trees once grew on the sea shore," explained Darwin, "See, crouch down here, and I'll show you what I mean."

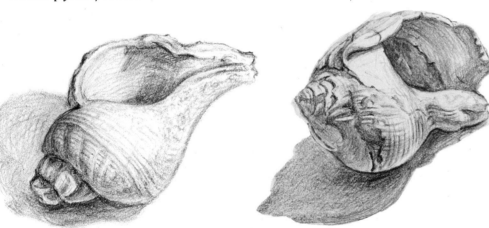

Fusus noachinus

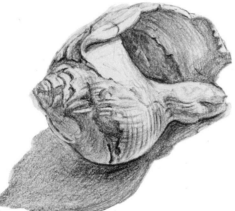

Gastridium cepa

Monoceros ambiguus

Pecten paranensis

Crepidula gregaria

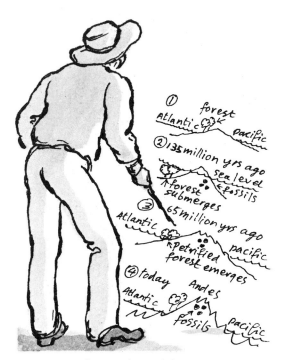

He grasped a stick and began to scratch rough pictures in the dust.

"Let us look at a cross-section of SOUTH AMERICA many millions of years ago. Here is a pine forest growing near the coast. Here is the Atlantic Ocean and here is the Pacific.

Now the ice age is over. The ice caps have melted and the level of the oceans has risen. Our pine forest is completely submerged.

As the earth cools, its crust contracts. This goes on all the time causing upheavals of layer upon layer of rocks. Such pressure causes faults in the earth's surface. The rocks tip upwards to form mountain ridges, volcanoes and earthquakes result. See how the picture is changing?

Here we are in the present. Endless movements of the earth's crusts have thrown the *Andes* range thousands of metres above sea level. Flows of lava cover the rocks. See how the sea has receded eroding the lava-stream slopes with its powerful tides. See the mud and shingle banks of the *Santa Cruz* river deposited as the sea withdrew. Do you remember how we saw all this during our journey up the river?"

"You can tell all this just from a few fossils and a patch of dead trees?" asked Ben wide-eyed.

"From the fossils and rocks and the shape of the land. You see, rocks can tell a very exciting story, Ben, almost as if they were speaking to you from the past."

The modern theory of the formation of the Andes

The theory Darwin developed on this expedition linked all his observations plausibly. Modern research, using sophisticated instruments and measuring techniques, have revealed more facts which do not accord with Darwin's original idea. The map below demonstrates the modern theory of how some mountain ranges, including the Andes, have been formed.

The earth is rather like a gigantic cracked egg. The broken pieces of 'shell' are called 'plates' because they resemble huge dinner plates, which fit together like a crazy football. Just inside the cracked shell is a very hot layer of toffee-like substance on which the plates slide about; as they push and pull at each other, oceans are created, continents moved and mountains thrown up.

The Andes, which so excited Darwin, have been and still are being, formed by two plates crushing together; a small one called the Nazca plate, and a much larger one, the South American plate. Where these two meet, the small plate is constantly forced under the larger one, and the land is built up to form the Andes. Volcanoes are also activated and they add volcanic rock to the mountains. This is a gradual and continual process. The earth's surface is changing all the time.

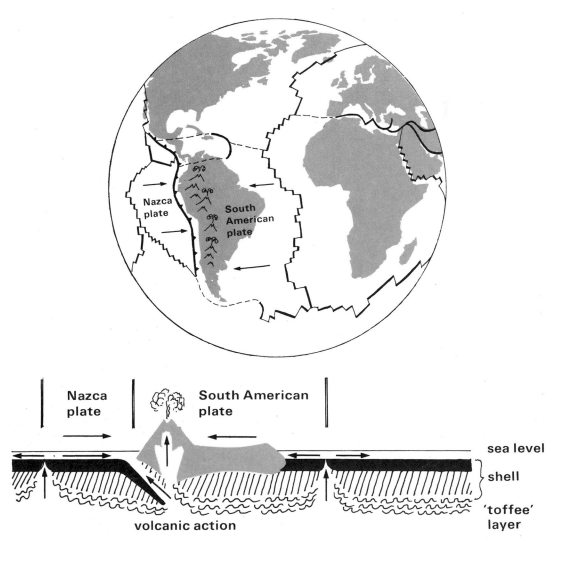

July 1834

It was now late summer 1834 and the crew of the Beagle made preparations to spend the next twelve months or so charting the west coast of SOUTH AMERICA in the same way that they had mapped the east coast during the previous year. Darwin was quite free to make his excursions into the mountains in search of material.

One such trip took him to the summit of the highest mountain in the *Andes* chain, the *Campana* or *Bell*. Below him, CHILE stretched out like a map. It was a long, narrow country bordered by the Pacific Ocean and the mountains. To his right, deep river gullies carved by mountain torrents forged their way to the green, coastal plains and the sea. To his left the snow-capped barrier known as the *Cordillera* rose like a high, impenetrable wall. All around lay scattered volcanic rocks, blown from the now dormant cones, and all so moss-free and shiny that Darwin could tell that eruptions had taken place quite recently.

On one journey, Darwin was approaching a village when he witnessed a swarm of locusts in action. Hearing a strange humming noise behind him, like the approach of a turbulent wind, Darwin turned his horse to find the sky darkened with a great rust-coloured cloud of smoke. The locust swarm was approaching at about ten to fifteen miles an hour in a thick column which rose up some thousand metres from the ground.

Locusts settled in dense blankets on

every morsel of green foliage and stripped it bare in seconds. The villagers ran out and lit fires, hoping the smoke would deter the insects, then, seeing that that had failed, they began to beat the ground and bushes with brooms. The swarm passed on relentlessly leaving a scene of complete desolation behind it.

That night, while sleeping rough in a neighbouring village, Darwin woke to feel something crawling unhurriedly over his body. It was a black and yellow mottled vinchuca bug, a soft, wingless insect almost three centimetres long. It had settled upon him in a thin and thirsty condition but in the space of ten minutes had drawn so much blood through its sucker that it was quite round and bloated. Darwin sprang up in disgust and cracked a shoe on the revolting bloodsucker. He had provided the insect with a rare treat, for one quenching feast would have lasted it up to four months.

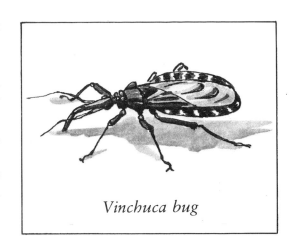

Vinchuca bug

Ben soon felt at home in the mountains. He learned to pick his path through the high passes as cautiously as a mule. But one day when scaling a perpendicular cliff face, choosing hand holds among the scarred, notched rocks, one hand grasped a loose chunk of bird dung and he crashed several feet to the ledge below.

"What the..." he swore, brushing down the raw graze on his ankle. A fierce, yellow eye stared down at him. The condor flicked its head sharply and its vivid red wattle shook with indignation. Huge claws grasped the rock edge defying him to climb again, and an enormous black-feathered body topped with a full white ruff emphasised the haughty, unforgiving glare.

"Come down gently, Ben," advised Darwin, "while the bird is still as surprised as you. I can see two large white eggs not far away on the ledge and I suspect it will regard you as a dangerous intruder once it has had time to think about it."

From a safer position, the two observed the wary bird.

"The eggs could roll off easily," commented Ben.

"Yes, condors don't build a nest, but choose an inaccessible spot high up in the mountain crags. There are probably more pairs around for the condor is quite a sociable bird and some twenty or thirty may share the same roosting territory."

"It's got the eyes and claws of a real killer," shuddered Ben.

"Those sharp eyes are for watching events on the ground as it circles high in the sky. The claws are for ripping flesh from the bones of its carrion prey. Apart from a lamb or a baby goat it rarely kills

its own food, preferring to let a puma do the hard work and take the pickings afterwards."

"This one looks fat enough, that's for sure."

"It probably gorged itself not so very long ago and was sitting quietly digesting its food when you came along. It won't eat again for several days."

The bird had watched them long enough. It backed away from the front of the ledge and in a few seconds they saw it soaring high above them in great spirals. Ben watched it carefully.

"It doesn't flap its wings," he said, "How does it stay up?"

"Just look at that enormous wing span. That's about two and a half metres wide and the largest wing feathers are fully spread to catch the warm currents of air rising from the ground. At that speed the bird needs to exert little effort to resist the pull of gravity."

"When do they learn to do this?" asked Ben.

"The young birds cannot fly for about a year. Even then they remain with their parents while they learn to hunt. They leave the nesting place when their white ruffs are fully grown, a sign that a young bird is mature."

Darwin and Ben descended the mountain, and later that day, saw a condor at even closer quarters. Their Chilean guides had found several roosting in trees near the camp and as the birds were very heavy sleepers, they had been able to climb up and noose a couple for their evening meal. At other times, the birds might be lured into an enclosure using a carcass. Once they were gorged with food they were unable to escape for their heavy bodies required a longer run for take-off.

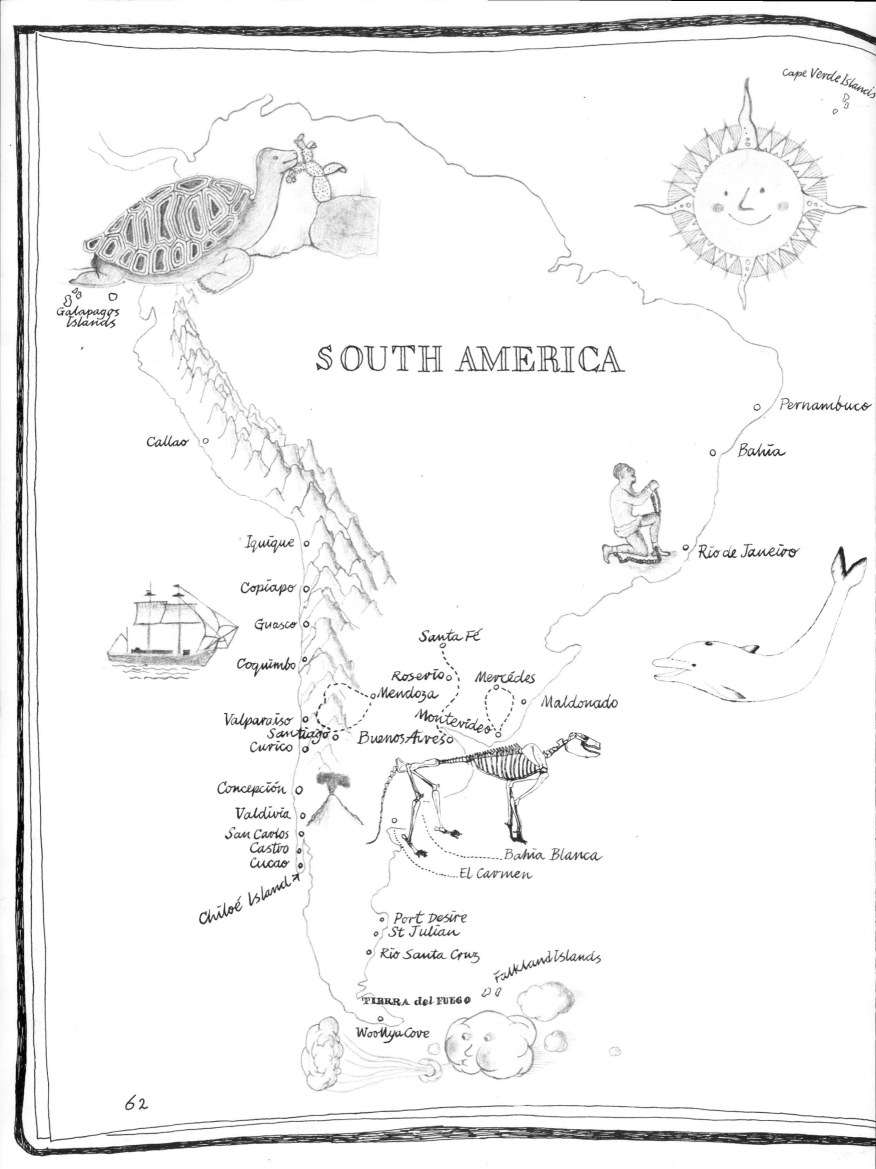

Cape Verde Islands

Galapagos
Islands

SOUTH AMERICA

Pernambuco

Bahia

Callao

Rio de Janeiro

Iquique

Copiapo

Guasco

Santa Fé

Coquimbo

Rosario

Mercédes

Mendoza

Maldonado

Valparaiso

Montevideo

Santiago

Buenos Aires

Curico

Concepción

Valdivia

Bahia Blanca

San Carlos

Castro

El Carmen

Cucao

Chiloé Island

Port Desire

St Julian

Rio Santa Cruz

Falkland Islands

TIERRA del FUEGO

Woollya Cove

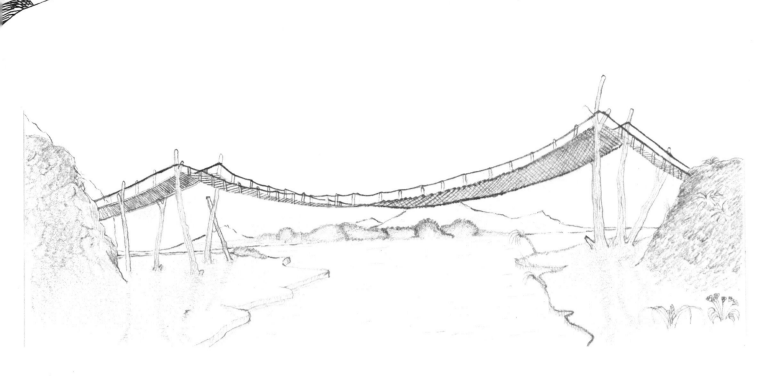

Climbing in the Cordilleras, Mr. Darwin and I came upon a great heap of stones and boulders, two such tipped one against the other in the manner of a high arch. Mr. Darwin immediately said it marked an Indian grave and we set about hunting for remains. But whether the bones had dried to dust or been borne off to the ancient tribal burial grounds, we could not tell, for we found nothing.

They pride themselves so hereabouts upon their bridges that Mr. Darwin said we could safely cross a turbulent river using a suspended bridge made of hide. Bridge indeed. It was fair he should go over first and the mule second, for I doubted either would reach the far side. The bridge was made of interlaced thongs, the road part being nothing but bundles of twigs hatched together very loosely and often in holes. I could stare down dizzily between my feet and see the distant ravine below. Then as we went, all three in careful file, the bridge swayed fearfully from side to side with the shift of our feet.

We joined the Beagle to chart the southernmost islands of the CHONOS ARCHIPELAGO and there, on a bleak shore, came upon five wild castaways who had wandered fifteen months in expectation of being delivered. They'd seen no living soul in all that time but had cheered themselves by keeping a tally of the days and maintaining good health and fitness on a diet of seal meat, shellfish and wild celery. Mr. Darwin said it was lucky we found them else they might have wandered on that lonely shore till they died; but for my part, I would count it good sport to live by my wits, there being plentiful fruits to gather.

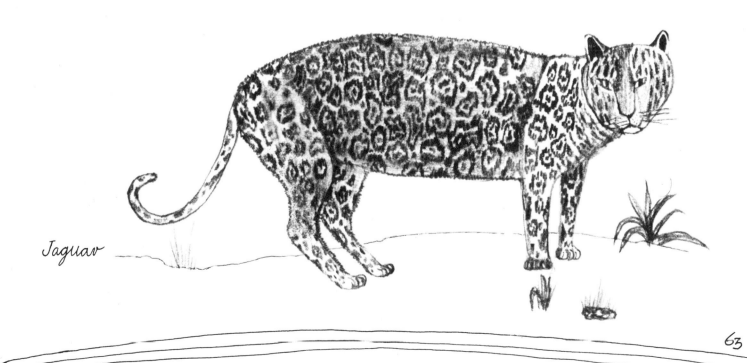

Jaguar

20th February 1835

On 20th February 1835, Darwin and Ben went ashore near the town of *Valdivia* where they experienced a frightening shaking and rocking of the ground beneath their feet which left them giddy and helpless for several minutes. On board the Beagle the crew reported that the boat had jolted with a heavy shock as if it had hit bottom.

Not until two weeks later, when they sailed northwards, did they realise they had had a lucky escape. The earthquake that had rocked over four hundred miles of the Chilean coast had done immeasurable damage. In the port of *Talcahuano* they found the town razed to the ground, debris scattered everywhere, dead animals lying with uprooted trees, household furniture with torn roofs. The smell of death and decay hung over the cracked and twisted streets where bewildered inhabitants rooted through the rubble for some fragmented reminder of their former lives.

The earthquake had come without warning, a series of convulsive, juddering shocks that made the ground open and close repeatedly in wide chasms. The earth had seemed to twist and churn to the echoes of a dry, grating noise. The sea had receded leaving ships high and dry in the bay, then, with all its force bottled up, it had swept inland in a series of great tidal

waves, each larger and more destructive than the last. The sea had risen in a boiling black whirlpool as if the floor of the ocean had cracked open and was sucking in and spewing out its contents. Great clouds of sulphurous smoke drifted off the sea mingling with the smothering dust and stifling heat.

The town of *Concepcion* was demolished in six seconds. Huge rocks bombarded the town from the slopes above, only to be swallowed up, along with the debris, by gaping holes which suddenly opened up in the ground. The cathedral and every building for miles around were destroyed.

By the time Darwin arrived over three hundred subsequent shocks had occurred like a slowly dying echo of the main earthquake. Surely, thought Darwin, the earth that seemed so stable and so firm was not so at all. Beneath its hard crust it was a heaving liquid mass of molten rock capable of forcing its way to the surface and destroying thousands of years of man's labour in a matter of seconds. This was clearly how the earth had formed and shaped itself and the process was still going on.

A few weeks later Darwin and Ben crossed the *Cordillera* by way of the dangerous *Portillo Pass*. On one occasion they were climbing steadily up the mountainside, Ben leading the way astride the 'madrina', a canny little mare whose instinct and tinkling bell would lead mules and men alike by the safest, easiest route through the Pass. Ben's tanned legs swung to either side of her body, which was already weighed down with cargo almost equal to his weight. Suddenly he saw her ears prick up and felt her back tense. Her hooves clipped the rock and her pace slowed. Ben leaned forward to pat her. "Hey lady, what's up? What's upset you?"

Their Chilean guide moved forward, leaping lightly to a high rock and crouching low in his lookout. After a second he beckoned the two travellers to join him.

A puma was picking its way down the rocky slope, its back and head low to the ground. Darwin's group were downwind but the puma was unlikely to notice them since its whole being was tense and alert to the presence of its prey. A small group of guanaco grazed upon dry grassy tufts in the ravine some distance from the main herd and the sentinel eye of the herd leader.

The puma was scarcely ten yards away when it sprang. The guanoco, immediately alert, turned as one to rejoin the main herd, who, stirring into simultaneous action, began to gallop down the valley in long, springing strides. But the puma had singled out a younger, weaker animal. Within seconds it was upon its back and had knocked it violently to the ground so that its neck broke. The puma wasted no time. Alert to the wheeling condors overhead who had gathered as if from nowhere at the hint of a free meal, it fell upon the carcass. It ate its fill despite having to chase off the odd daring birds, then began to pull the remainder of the meal into the undergrowth.

"What's it doing?" asked Ben.

"It will bury the carcass under some bushes and lie guard over it, as well it might if it hopes to keep any more for itself," answered Darwin with a smile.

In these northern mountains Darwin discovered that the rock layers often bore veins of copper, iron, silver and gold. Numerous small mines had been set up high in the hills to work these deposits.

The Chilean miners worked continuously for three weeks and were then allowed a two day rest period during which they visited their families far below in the villages. The work was extremely hard. The miners were fed on beans and bread alone, were treated like beasts of burden and lived in draughty huts without comfort. The mines had no lifts so each man hauled the rock to the surface on his back. Loads amounted to more than a man's own weight and the ascent from the depths of the mine was made up a rough ladder of notched tree trunks.

The miners were severely punished if caught attempting to steal the gold ore. The value of the stolen gold would be deducted from the wages of each and every miner. By this clever device the owners made sure that each man kept a careful check upon his neighbour.

Mule trains carried the ore down to the hills where it was crushed and washed. A gentle current of water carried away the lighter dust particles leaving the precious metal at the bottom of the sluice.

On 12th July 1835, just two months before the Beagle was due to leave SOUTH AMERICA on its journey across the Pacific, Darwin sent off his last package of specimens. The parcels were bound for Professor Henslow in Cambridge and contained the last remaining natural history items collected throughout the continent. Now he was totally engrossed in the study of geology and looked forward to the remainder of the trip, especially the visit to the volcanic *Galapagos Islands*, for the work he would be able to do in that field.

"There," he said, dusting down his hands and regarding the closed crate with satisfaction, "that's the last of the animals and plants. I doubt there will be much to add to our collection in that field from now on."

He was quite wrong. Darwin's most important discoveries were yet to come.

After a two week journey, the Beagle arrived in the *Galapagos Islands,* a cluster of twelve small islands some four hundred miles off the coast of EQUADOR. From his geological observations in SOUTH AMERICA, Darwin could tell that the islands had been pushed up out of the sea by volcanic eruptions for they were formed entirely from volcanic rocks. The smaller islands were often no more than small cones rising above layer upon layer of black lava and fringed with beaches of black sand, but the larger ones rose inland to high peaks. Here the vegetation grew lusher and thicker as one climbed and the dormant craters sometimes contained small lakes of crystal clear water or, at very least, bubbling springs which thirsty animals had trodden into a muddy water hole.

But, as it happened, it was not the rocks but the plants and animals that offered most surprises, for although they resembled plants and animals to be found on the continent of America, they were, in fact, all quite different. Darwin was spellbound, for now he had new birds, plants, shells, insects and reptiles to study, none of which he had ever seen before.

There was not much time for the Beagle was due to depart for *Tahiti* in just four weeks. A quick survey of the whole Archipelago revealed that the picture was even more complicated, for not only were these species totally unknown to him, but each island seemed to possess its own types of those species. There was clearly some hard collecting and observing to do and choosing *James Island* on which to make an intense study, Darwin and Ben set off in a small rowing boat to set up camp there.

Part of the map from 'Narrative of the Surveying Voyages of His Majesty's Ships Adventure and Beagle' by Captain Fitzroy

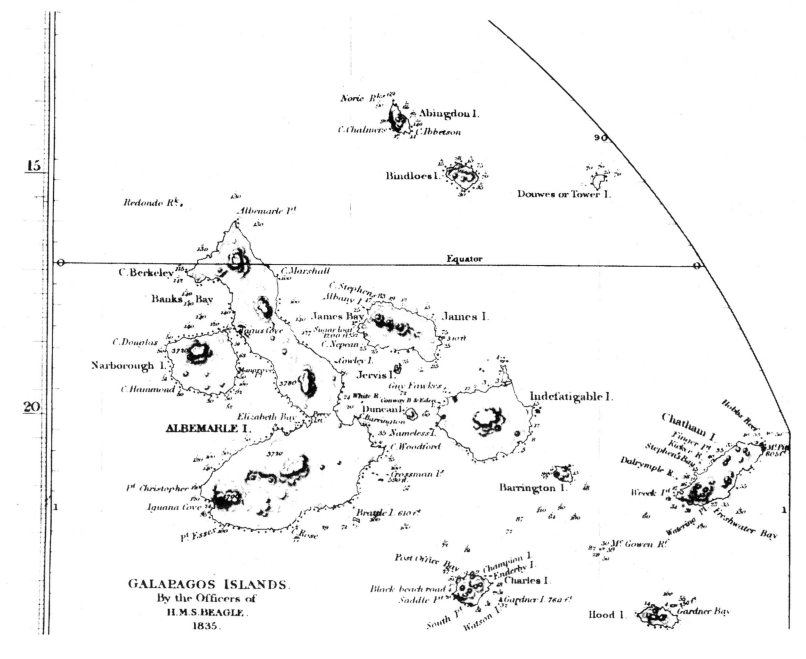

Marine iguana

One day they visited *Chatham Island*. They were able to beach the boat easily, but it was more difficult to find a foothold on the sharp, black rocks for they swarmed with thousands of enormous lizard-like creatures.

"Marine iguanas," said Darwin, "I hope they're not as fierce as they look."

"Ugly great brute," hissed Ben, "budge off there," and he stamped on the ground to frighten off a large specimen that lay stretched out in the sun, blocking his path. The creature raised its head and looked at Ben unblinkingly. It moved forward in a slow, sluggish gait, heaving itself over the rocks on its clawed limbs. "They aren't afraid," said Ben with some relief and he stamped his way on inland, often picking an iguana out of the way by its tail or rolling one over with his boot.

Darwin had picked one up and was examining it closely. It lay outstretched, over a metre long, in his arms, its blunted nose uplifted, while it made small nervous jerky movements up and down with its head. Its entire body was a dirty black, often patched with grey and crowned with a spine of jagged teeth that ran from the top of its head to the tip of its tail.

"What does it eat?" asked Ben, warily watching it sniff at Darwin's finger.

"Marine iguanas live on seaweed that grows at the bottom of the sea. You will see them swimming out in large shoals to the feeding grounds. They are powerful swimmers. Their legs tuck in to make a streamlined shape and they propel themselves along by swinging their tail and body in snake-like curves. Otherwise they

are happiest on land where they have no enemies, for their greatest predator is the shark."

"They remind me of those strange reptile-like dinosaurs you told me about at *Bahia Blanca*," said Ben, thinking back to their earlier meeting with prehistoric giants.

"That's sharp thinking," applauded Darwin. "This is the only true marine lizard in existence and the last of that line which started with those gigantic lizards of long ago."

The land iguanas inhabited the central islands of the Archipelago, preferring the higher damper parts of the volcanoes' slopes. Here they swarmed in the same great numbers as the marine iguana on the rocky shore.

The land iguana was a brownish-red colour with a yellow-orange stomach, altogether a muddier colour to help it blend with its background. However, it shared many of the habits of the marine species. It moved very slowly, crawling along on its short legs with its belly and tail dragging along behind, and often

stopped in the middle of its tracks to take a snooze. When frightened, it would lurch along at a near run making for the safety of its burrow, a shallow tunnel leading down into the softer sandstone of the region.

These creatures, like all the others on the *Galapagos Islands*, had few enemies and rarely showed any timidity when approached by man. They shared their meal of cactus or acacia leaves with tortoise and bird alike, often clambering up to eat the sour berries of the guayavita tree.

Darwin was eager to know if there were any giant tortoises on the island so one day he and Ben set out on a quest to find them. Following a well-beaten track uphill, they soon came across a huge, male tortoise lurching methodically up the path. Its neck was far outstretched as if it had caught the first scent of thirst-quenching water.

Darwin and the boy fell in step behind the animal, happy to slow down for a while and move at the tortoise's pace.
"Has it come far, Mr. Darwin?" asked Ben.
"About eight miles, I should think. Do you remember the dry, volcanic crater we passed earlier? I suspect several thousand tortoises inhabit that area, but that they all make the journey to the rich, green upper regions of the island from time to time to refresh themselves at the springs."

Although they were almost treading on the animal's tail, it seemed totally unaware that it was being followed.
"It's a solid, ugly thing," reflected Ben, "but it's sort of gentle and defenceless too."
"The natives believe they are totally deaf," said Darwin, "and I'm inclined to agree with them, but it's not defenceless by any means. Walk on ahead a little and you'll see what I mean."

Ben pulled alongside the tortoise then strode boldly on ahead. Immediately the animal let out a deep hiss and pulling its head and legs under its shell, it collapsed in a protective heap on the ground.

"Gosh," said Ben dropping to his knees and peering round the base of the shell, "That's real armour plating. How long do you think it'll stay like that?"

"We'll get it on its feet again," laughed Darwin. "Climb up astride the shell. Careful! It's slippy and you've no hand hold."

Once Ben was established in a straddled position, Darwin bent over and tapped the tortoise firmly on its rump. It responded like a trained beast of burden, rising up and bearing its passenger forward on a lurching, skiddering ride. It was a crazy, turbulent journey while it lasted but before long Ben had slid and rolled to the ground, leaving his untroubled steed to journey placidly on its way.

The two pushed ahead and soon reached the open clearing that marked the location of the springs. At first glance it seemed that the island's entire tortoise population had congregated there, some to nibble the overhanging foliage, the berries and lichens, and others to wallow lazily in the mud or suck up great, greedy gulps of water.

"Look at him then," said Ben, pointing to a huge specimen nearby.

"That's an old male," instructed Darwin. "They grow to the largest size of all. The males are larger than the females anyway, but you can also tell them by their longer tails. That one must weigh two hundred pounds and it would take a few strong fellows to lift it."

It was not difficult to watch the creatures at close quarters or to collect samples of each kind for they were all surprisingly tame. Clearly the animals had inhabited the islands for so long without any real interference from animal or human predators, that they did not know the meaning of fear. Their only enemies were the men from the American whaling boats who made visits to these islands from time to time, They would carry out a wholesale massacre of giant tortoises, for the meat was very tasty when cooked in its shell. The animals were quite defenceless once they were tipped over on their backs.

Even the birds showed no alarm. They would alight on Darwin's outstretched arm or settle on Ben's head as if this was the natural place to perch, although all round the men of the Beagle were knocking them down and killing them with sticks. Even on *Charles Island*, the one inhabited spot, where hundreds of convicts farmed and hunted, the birds had learned little caution. Darwin wondered how long it would be before this trusting instinct vanished and the birds took to the skies at the slightest movement just as they did at home.

1 *Short-eared owl*
2 *Galapagos hawk*
3 *Galapagos dove*
4 *Penguin*
5 *Sea lion*
6 *Flightless cormorant*
7 *Yellow warbler*
8 *Lava lizard*
9 *Mockingbird*

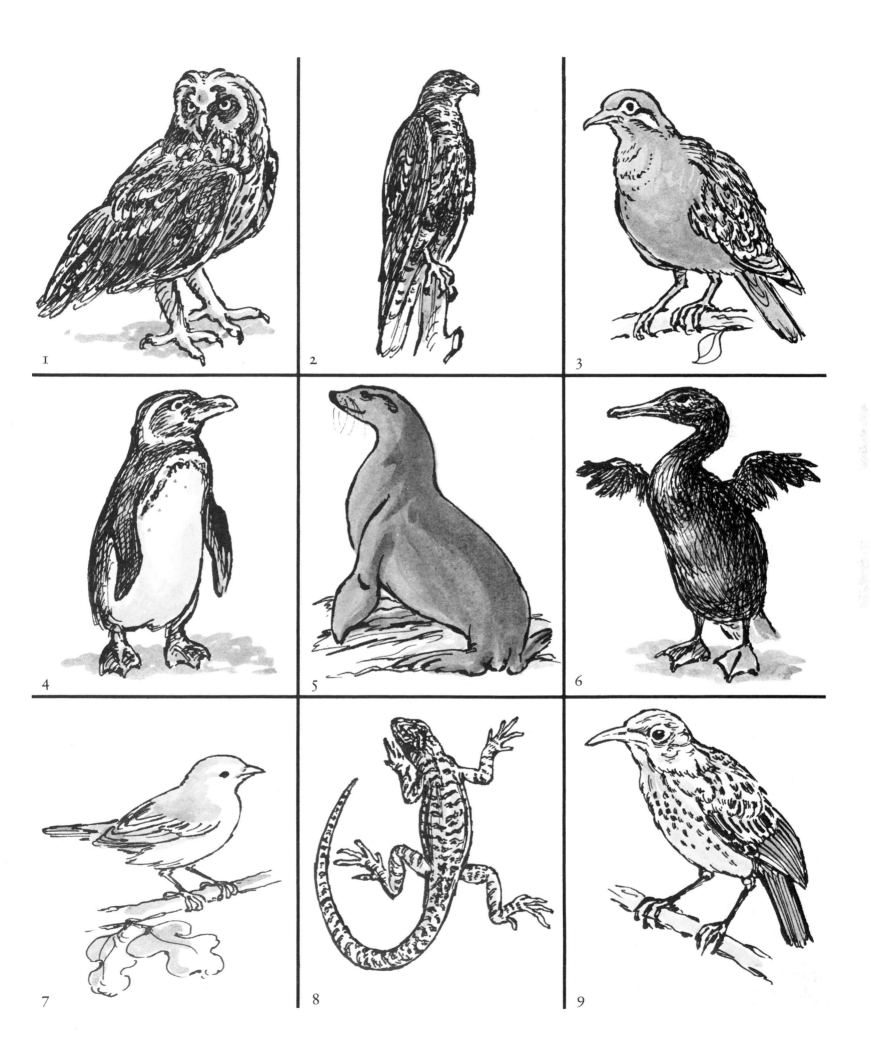

Fortunately for Darwin, it had been agreed that the crew of the Beagle should help him in the *Galapagos* as their stay was to be short, so now they were busily gathering specimens by the dozen from every island in the Archipelago. When he came to sort through the great pile of finches laid out on deck, he soon noticed striking differences between those brought from one island and those from another. All the finches were of more or less the same size, all had short tails. All were reported to build nests with roofs over them, to lay four eggs, white in colour with pink spots and Darwin remembered that he and Ben had heard them chirruping in a very unmusical way.

But there the similarities ended. Some had black feathers whilst others had dull green, some had strong thick beaks and others sharp, fine ones; some nested in trees, some on the ground and some on the forked leaves of cactus plants.

The shape of the beak showed clearly what the birds ate. The strong beaks cracked nuts and seeds, the finer ones picked up insects; one finch even used a cactus spike to winkle insects and grubs out of holes. Some finches had wide fruit-eating beaks and still others with narrow beaks fed on flowers and leaves.

Darwin puzzled on this for some time. It was probable that all fourteen species of finch here in the *Galapagos Islands* had descended from a seed-eating ground finch of America. Having flown far afield and settled on these islands, the descendants of the birds had slowly adapted to their new environment. On those islands where the nuts and seeds were plentiful the finches had changed hardly at all, but where the diet was fruit or insects the birds had been forced to adapt or starve.

Finches: contrasts in development of beaks to suit different eating habits.

Large finch

Medium finch

Vegetarian finch

Large insectivorous finch

Small finch

Sharp-beaked finch

Large insectivorous finch

Small insectivorous finch

Cactus finch

Large cactus finch

Woodpecker finch

Mangrove finch

a) Large ground finch has a large beak to crack and eat a variety of hard seeds.

b) Warbler finch has a slender beak to catch mainly small exposed insects.

Warbler finch

Cocos finch

Movement of continents and evolution of mammals in South America

The land connection between North and South America was broken throughout much of the Tertiary period, leaving South America as an island continent. When this split occurred the animals living in South America were left to evolve in isolation for millions of years producing many unique and bizzare forms. Three major groups of mammals were involved, the notoungulates, the edentates and the marsupials. Notoungulates, a group which included a wide variety of large herbivorous forms, became totally extinct during the Pleistocene, but numerous kinds of edentate and marsupial still survive in South America today.

Although there was no direct land connection re-established until the late Pliocene period, from the Oligocene onwards several kinds of small mammal found their way to South America from the North via islands between the two continents, for example the caviomorph rodents (guinea pig family) and the New World monkeys. Following the great interchange of animals between northern and southern continents during the Pleistocene, nearly all of the larger southern species became extinct, though some such as the giant sloths and glyptodon probably survived late enough to have been seen by early man in the Americas.

This modern chart shows what has been learned since Darwin's death, about the development of mammals in South America.

How the land developed   *The effect the land changes had on animals*

QUATERNARY PERIOD
CAENOZOIC ERA

PLEISTOCENE about 2 million years ago

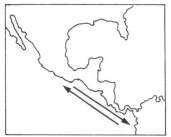

Land bridge joined North and South America together. Major migrations of mammals took place in both directions.

NORTH to SOUTH

Advanced *herbivores i.e. Mastodon, Hippidion.

Advanced *carnivores i.e. Sabre toothed cats, Jaguars, Wolves, Foxes.

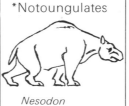

SOUTH to NORTH

*Edentates i.e. Glyptodon, Armadillos, Giant ground sloths.

*Marsupials i.e. Opossums.

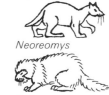

*Rodents i.e. Porcupines.

TERTIARY PERIOD
CAENOZOIC ERA

PLIOCENE about 7 million years ago.
MIOCENE about 26 million years ago.
OLIGOCENE about 38 million years ago.

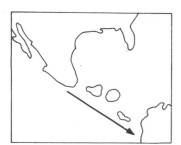

During the Oligocene Miocene and Pliocene, islands developed between N. and S. America.

Some Miocene mammals of South America

*Notoungulates	*Edentates	*Marsupials	Immigrants *Rodents
Nesodon	Stegotherium	Borhyaena	Neoreomys
Homalodotherium	Hapalops	Prothylacynus	Steiromys
	Propalaeohoplophorus	Necrolestes	*Primates Homunculus

Certain forms of Rodent and Primate mammals migrated from North to South America.

EOCENE 50 million years ago.
South America became an island.

Unique forms of these three main groups developed in South America.

PALAEOCENE 70 million years ago.
North and South America were still joined together.

Edentate, Marsupial and Notoungulate mammals, lived in both North and South America.

MESOZOIC ERA

CRETACEOS 100 million years ago.
North and South America were joined together.

Dinosaurs dominant, small mammals exist. (Dinosaurs became extinct at the end of the Cretaceous nobody knows why.)

* Edentates-*toothless*, Marsupials-*pouched*, Notoungulates-*extinct Herbivores*, Rodents-*gnawers*, Primates-*apes and monkeys*, Herbivores-*plant eaters*, Carnivores-*flesh eaters*.

to be read from the bottom upwards

Ben asked, "Did many starve? Those that didn't change quickly enough and couldn't eat properly?"

"That's difficult to say," said Darwin. "It seems clear that most species produce too many offspring so that those young individuals who vary in some beneficial way from the rest, will have the better chance of surviving. Survival of the fittest, you might say."

"So the moth who looked most like a scorpion survived and the beetle that looked like a poisonous fruit." Ben paused. "And that octopus, you know, the one that changed colour; all their predators left them alone."

"That's it! And when they in turn hatched young, the ones who looked most like their parents or who were even better examples of camouflage would be the ones most likely to survive. So gradually the species would get better and better at surviving."

"And that's what the poor mastodons and megatheriums were so hopeless at," remembered Ben.

"Yes. They couldn't adapt quickly enough when new, fierce predators arrived in their midst."

Once more the poop cabin was piled with skins and stuffed animals, insects in pill boxes, shells, pickled specimens in jars, feathers, rocks and page upon page of scribbled notes.

"We'd best get another crate packed off to Mr. Henslow," said Ben, eyeing the mess dubiously.

"No, it can wait now," argued Darwin, "after all we will be home in six months if all goes well, and I don't want to risk these important specimens getting lost or delayed. You've worked hard, Ben, and I'll always be grateful to you for your help, but it's time you took a holiday now. The work of the Beagle is done except for a little detailed time-keeping here and there, and my work is almost done too. We're making good headway now across the Pacific and the weather's fine and sunny. I suggest you leave me to my writing in this cramped little den and take yourself up on the yard arm with your sketch pad. I'll be grateful for any drawings you can add to my researches, you know."

Darwin had judged right. A holiday feeling had taken over the crew of the Beagle and all thoughts of home-sickness were put aside as the ship sped towards *Tahiti* and home.

The surviving mammals Ben and Darwin might have seen.

EDENTATES

Ant-eaters

two-toed　　　*tamandua*　　　*giant*

Sloths

two-toed　　　*three-toed*

Armadillos (9 genera)

little　　　*nine-banded*　　　*giant*

MARSUPIALS

Opossums

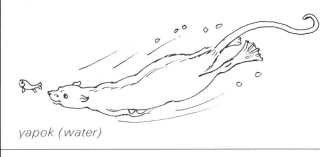

American

yapok (water)

murine

They arrived at *Tahiti* on 15th November 1835 to a rapturous welcome. Dozens of canoes steered by well-built, bronzed men came out to greet them while a great crowd of men, women and children waved and cheered from the shore. The women, often wearing only a brightly coloured sarong, had flowers fastened through their pierced ears and wore garlands of coconut leaves on their heads to shade their eyes. The men were lean, tall and well-proportioned. Many wore white skirts tucked into their sarongs while others revealed fine floral tattoos on their bodies, feet and hands.

The villagers had built their homes on the narrow strip of low ground that was sheltered by the high mountains behind and the coral reef in front. Inside the reef, the water was calm and shallow and the men could fish easily with the nets or spears. On land, every patch of available ground had been planted with tropical fruits and vegetables, bananas, oranges, yams, sweet potato, sugar cane and pineapple.

On a trip into the mountains Darwin and his native guides travelled light. They caught fish in pools, plucked fruit from the trees, built their bivouac from bamboos and banana leaves and drank from the mountain springs.

Darwin and Ben were often invited into Tahitian homes to buy tropical shells, the natives greeting them with odd words and phrases of English learned from the missionaries and foreign traders who had settled there. Several families might live together in one large, airy wooden hut, an arced framework of light timber resting on slender posts. A thatch of palm leaves helped to keep the interior cool.

Once they joined a group of children gathered round a bonfire on the beach. By the flickering firelight they sang haunting songs and cast swaying shadows on the sea.

The return trip to the ship, which was moored in deep water out in the bay, was a perilous operation. Despite the full moon that lit up the sea and the calm, competent manner in which their native helmsman steered the small boat sharply to right and left, it seemed to Darwin that the channels through the coral reef were haphazard and very narrow and he expected to hear the grating sound of ripping timber at every second.

By daylight the reef was a different matter. At low tide, the coral was exposed in many places, and wearing tough footwear to withstand the sharp, rough shells, Darwin and Ben set off to collect samples. Darwin explained that although coral looked like chunks of dead rocks and much of the lower part of the reef would, in fact, be composed of dead coral, the surface and side of the reef contained living creatures called polyps.

"Imagine the first polyp arriving here. It finds warm water at at least twenty degrees centigrade, and shallow sea which gets full sunlight at low tide, so it secretes a hard substance called calcium

carbonate or limestone and anchors itself firmly to a hard rock on the sea bed. Then it secretes more limestone to form a protective coating over its surface.

"It leaves one small opening at the top as a mouth. In daylight or at low tide it is inactive, but at night stinging tentacles reach out underwater to paralyse and catch passing prey. The tentacles draw the food towards the mouth and into the stomach of the polyp where it is digested. A healthy polyp will reproduce by budding as if it was growing another stalk through its side wall. Coral is formed by a continual process of budding so that a great colony of polyps is formed, all joined to another in an ever-growing coral reef."

"They're lovely colours," said Ben with his artist's eye, as he hammered off small brittle pieces of pink, white, mauve and yellow coral."

"And lovely shapes," said Darwin, "for you will see that although most of the reef is composed of this staghorn type, there are small clusters of different shaped corals here and there."

Queen Pomare

88

Today we got ourselves fancied out and went ashore on the King's business. Captain Fitzroy had called upon the chiefs and their Queen to attend a court to investigate a dastardly piece of piracy, and he was intent to show a stern, scolding manner to one and all.

The court was held in the chapel, the chiefs sitting upright in the pews, having removed their straw hats upon the arrival of Queen Pomare, and her few attendants. She seemed a fat, plain-looking woman to me, though not old, and no one seemed to show her much respect, except Captain Fitzroy who went up straightaway and shook her by the hand.

He said it was a bad affair to rob such a ship as the Truro, and that the promised recompense of 2,853 dollars had still not been paid. He said His Majesty of Great Britain was very angry and would take steps to recover his money if it was not soon delivered.

The Queen said nothing (out of a bad conscience, Mr. Darwin said), for it was her relatives who had stolen all. But the chiefs rose with great dignity and said all the money would be found there and then, payment to be made in rich shells and coins. Captain Fitzroy told them they were honest, wise men and that the Queen would do better next time to follow their advice.

Soon after this we left TAHITI, and set sail for NEW ZEALAND, passing many small islands on the way. Many of the islands were inhabited, if only by a small group of natives or an English trader and his men. Mr. Darwin told me that others had been discovered by much earlier voyagers, who had crossed the ocean in simple, dug-out canoes, watching the flight direction of passing sea-birds overhead, shags, boobies and other short-winged birds. These seldom flew more than a hundred miles from land since they preferred to roost on dry land each night. In this way, the intrepid traveller had only to follow them to know he would eventually reach land of some sort or another.

Our officers, of course, had far superior navigational instruments, and by mid-December, we made a safe landfall at NORTH ISLAND, NEW ZEALAND. Mr. Darwin, who is very homesick, loves the island because it reminds him of home. He delights in the neat houses, with their 'English' gardens, the farms and villages surrounded by fields of golden corn and the forests of tall Kauri pines.

Today Mr. Darwin and I managed to join hands round the trunk of a giant Kauri pine whose trunk measured thirty-three feet in circumference, a gigantic column of smooth timber with branches sprouting rather weakly at the top. We also searched for remains of the extinct Moa a great flightless bird that could stand more than nine feet high. Mr. Darwin says that other hunters had found bones and feathers but no one had seen one of these birds alive.

extinct Moa bird

From NEW ZEALAND it was a short journey to *Sydney* in AUSTRALIA. This great city had sprung from nothing in under fifty years and for one very good reason; it was one of the receiving stations for the shiploads of convicts exiled from England to Australia as punishment. The convicts provided a vast labour force and farmers and business men alike were growing rich at their expense. Once a convict had served his sentence, he too was free to buy land, or labour on his own behalf.

To Darwin, Sydney seemed a hotbed of greed and dishonesty. For this reason he made his escape into the lush hills and valleys of the *Blue Mountains* to visit a large sheep farm called Walerawang. The land stretched away to the horizon in softly undulating hills, rarely broken by more than a single twisted eucalyptus tree or burnt tree stump.

Few birds or animals frequented such open countryside. Constant hunting with over-zealous English greyhounds had driven all the kangaroos and emus away. Indeed apart from a few beautiful parrots or white cockatoos, Darwin saw little of interest beside a platypus which was diving playfully from the banks of a river.

It seemed as if the white colonists had driven every native thing away, including the aborigine who often thoughtlessly gave up his land for the sake of a few cheap gifts, a little milk and meat, and the occasional use of a hunting dog.

All this made Darwin increasingly anxious to get home, back to his father who had financed him throughout the voyage, back to his sisters who had sent regular letters bearing all the family news, and back to his cousin, Emma Wedgwood for whom he had a special affection.

"Can't say as *I* feel very homesick," commented Ben, "Since I ain't got a home to go back to. I might as well stay here and become a wealthy sheep farmer."

"Nonsense," chided Darwin, "you have many friends on board the Beagle, not least Captain Fitzroy and myself. We have had some conversation about your future, Ben, and I promise you, we'll see you get a good position when we get back to England."

But now, just because everyone was wishing time away, the days seemed to drag more slowly despite the series of holiday-like visits they were making to islands en route.

6th March 1836

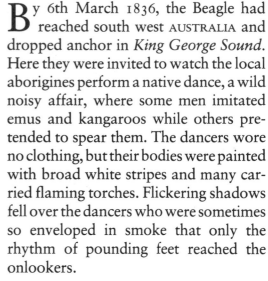

By 6th March 1836, the Beagle had reached south west AUSTRALIA and dropped anchor in *King George Sound.* Here they were invited to watch the local aborigines perform a native dance, a wild noisy affair, where some men imitated emus and kangaroos while others pretended to spear them. The dancers wore no clothing, but their bodies were painted with broad white stripes and many carried flaming torches. Flickering shadows fell over the dancers who were sometimes so enveloped in smoke that only the rhythm of pounding feet reached the onlookers.

On the *Cocos Islands* in the Indian Ocean there was more dancing and singing by the native Malay women. There was also a great deal to occupy Darwin.

On these remote islands there was little variety of food. Men and animals had to adapt their diet to what was available and this led to some unusual sights. Strangest of all were the giant robber crabs whose two pincers were so strong that they could tear off the fibre from a coconut, hammer it open through one of the weaker eye-holes in the shell, then bore out the fleshy part of the nut using a pair of narrow pincers located at their rear end.

The natives warned of great clams that would fasten round a swimmer's leg and hold him fast till he drowned. They showed Darwin fish that ate coral and dogs that dived for fish, and even rats who nested in the top fronds of palm trees for greater safety.

By April they had reached *Mauritius,* a truly undiscovered and unspoilt island near MADAGASCAR and the African coast. Darwin was the honoured guest of the island's Surveyor General, in fact, so honoured that he made the journey back to the ship on the back of his host's personal elephant.

But now, they were rounding the *Cape of Good Hope,* and urging the Beagle homewards at full speed.

But there was to be a further delay. Fitzroy was unhappy about some of the early coastal readings taken at the beginning of the voyage, and he turned the ship across the Atlantic again towards BRAZIL to make a quick check. How every minute dragged! After five years of intermittent sea-sickness and long stretches of being cooped up with the Captain or the officers sharing the poop cabin, the thought of long walks over the Shropshire hills, of open green fields and clear bird songs, made Darwin sick with impatience.

"I wonder if I have changed," he thought, "whether I shall fit into a family of newly-married sisters and young nieces and nephews? I wonder if they will find me a dull, steady, sort of chap now, poring over my natural history specimens and notes. And will my father accept my new career, for I mean to go on studying until I have made greater sense of all I have seen? Indeed, if I can contribute one idea to man's knowledge of the natural world I shall be happy."

But first Darwin had a debt of friendship to repay. Ben and he had shared many adventures and had become good friends. Over the duration of the voyage Ben had developed from a gangly youth to a well-proportioned young man, and with this maturity had come great powers of concentration, intelligence and artistic talent.

So it was that some months later, Darwin travelled north to Scotland and met Ben at a pre-arranged spot in the busy city of Edinburgh. Guiding his protegé through the bustle of traffic and people, he halted at last before the wrought iron railings of a tall, dignified house. Attached to the gate pillar was an embossed plaque bearing the words, "John Bartholomew: reputable map and chartmaker."

Mr. Bartholomew, it turned out, had been very interested in the sketches that Darwin had brought to his attention. He had praised the neatness and accuracy of eye of the young Ben Sweet, and had willingly offered to accept him as an apprentice engraver in his newly-formed workshop in Edinburgh.

"I'm going to work here?" gasped Ben. "Making maps like Captain Fitzroy kept in the locker room?"

"If you would like to, of course," Darwin assured him. "Mr. Bartholomew has a great interest in our voyage in the Beagle, Ben, and will undoubtedly listen avidly to your accounts. What is more, he plans to obtain permission from the Admiralty to produce maps and charts based on our findings and you will be of invaluable help to him there. Well, it's up to you, Ben. I wish you luck and every success."

"You always told me something great would come from our efforts, Mr. Darwin," glowed Ben, "though I never guessed I'd find such a chance. But the greatest success, will be yours, sir, for you opened my eyes to a world of marvels and understanding and others will wonder at your words and listen to your teachings, that I know . . . and don't forget now," Ben's face broke into a smile, "I'll always be a willing companion when you venture out on a spot of beetle collecting."